DIVORCE WITH JOY

DIVORCE WITH JOY

A DIVORCE ATTORNEY'S
GUIDE TO HAPPY EVER AFTER©

Joy Ragan, Esq

Contents

I dedicate this book to the souls that saved me,
my Duggan and Jack, with all my love.

ACKNOWLEDGEMENTS

TO the One who brought me through this journey, the One who has become my greatest friend: thank you for teaching me true love. My greatest hope is to glorify You.

To my family: Thank you for allowing me to tell our story. I am immensely grateful for your courage and understanding. To Mike especially: thank you for walking in this partnership to raise our beautiful boys. You will always have my deepest gratitude.

To my Board of Directors: You have been my glue when I was falling apart, my heart when I was too broken to feel, my good sense when I threw it out the window, and my challengers when I was too scared to keep going. Namaste.

To my coaches, editors and all those who touched this book in its formation: I thank you and hope to have made you proud.

*"The Journey of a Thousand Miles
Begins with One Single Step"*

Happy Ever After

There is a saying among attorneys. "In criminal defense cases you have 'bad' people suddenly on their best behavior. In family law cases, you have 'good' people suddenly on their worst behavior." Often people say divorce brings out the worst in us. A divorce is a catalyst. It is a challenging time in life that will bring about change. The change, however, doesn't have to be the kind that brings out the worst in us. Divorce can be a time of transition to generate a positive change in our lives. It can facilitate our happy ever after. During the time when our marriages are in shambles, we can transform ourselves and our family into a better version of us. During the break down of our marriages, we can rebuild better lives, married or divorced. If we use this separation time to bring out the best in us, I believe often our marriages can be saved. Understand that right now, at the beginning of the process you don't have to know whether or not you want to get divorced. The beginning stages of the journey are the same whether you ultimately get divorced or work to save the marriage. When you do the work in the beginning, even if you ultimately move forward with divorce, your divorce will be happy, healthy, productive and monumentally less expensive, both financially and emotionally. Either way, at the end of the process, your family can be healed.

We are not victims of a broken legal system. We don't have to accept that the breakdown of a marriage is an unyielding trauma. It is our choice whether this change we are about to experience is positive or negative change. If you insist the change be positive, it will be positive. If you insist, through your words, actions and perspective, that the change be negative, it will be negative. I believe there is a place for common sense and spiritual awakening in the divorce process. If you choose to share that belief, it will be an amazing (if at times difficult) journey. This book can help you make choices that will benefit your family: from how to deal with your spouse; to how to select an attorney; to how to experience the process from separation through divorce; to moving on as a family after divorce. If you choose to share my common sense approach with a measure of spiritual awakening, you may be able to save your marriage. But, even if you make the decision to divorce, your family will thrive. Either way, your family can be saved and you will live your happy ever after.

Is this book written for men or women?

Yes! This book is universal. It has practical tools that apply no matter the gender of the reader. Granted, much of this book is my perspective and, by necessity, my perspective is female. However, I represent men and women equally in divorces. My professional perspective is very gender neutral. I spent many years growing up with my Father. And, like many men, I was not "in touch" with my feelings; nor was I a very emotional person when I reached the point where my marriage was in shambles. At that point, I thought I could "figure" things out and control outcomes and do all the things that men also tend to think they can do. The process has led me to a very different place. As a result, I believe I have a perspective that can resonate with both genders equally.

For example, let me just play "devil's advocate". Let's say that you (as a man) don't identify with anything you read in this book. Let's say you get to the end and you still think it is gibberish. You can bet, even if you don't identify with it, your spouse probably does. Wouldn't it be beneficial to gain some insight on her perspective? Don't you think such insight may help you move forward in a more productive way, married or divorced? If all you get out of this book is some insight on how to better interact with your spouse, and thus be a better Father, you have not wasted your time. Nor have I wasted mine. Therefore, the book is not for men or for women exclusively, it is for people who find their marriage is a mess and their relationships unmanageable. It is for people who are willing to open their minds and hearts to a different way of experiencing the process which may or may not lead to divorce.

Is it worth spending the money for this book?

My intention is for those considering separating from their spouse or otherwise contemplating divorce to buy this book as a first step. I think if you read it before making any big moves, you may view the situation differently and move forward in a more productive way. This book is, essentially, an extended version of information you should receive in an initial consultation with an attorney. Such consultations cost between $250 and $400. When you compare the price of this book to the cost of an initial consultation, it is a great value.

In an initial consultation, the client receives a massive amount of information in a short amount of time. It is often too much for the client to fully absorb. Having information in book form allows you to go through it at your own pace so you can grasp and apply the concepts. Plus, people often delay seeing an attorney because they view it as a big step. Maybe you aren't ready to take the step of making an appointment with an attorney and the formality of a consultation, but you want basic information on how things may look going forward. This book allows you to do just that. You can read it in the privacy of your own home. You also have the comfort of knowing that this book comes from a good place. It is the perspective of an attorney who has absolutely no ulterior motives. You don't have to wrestle with the thought that maybe you can't trust the attorney with whom you are consulting because that attorney may just want to sell you on a divorce to make money.

This book is designed to help you spend as little money on attorneys as possible. If you move through the process as outlined in the book, you may end up not getting divorced at all. But, if you get divorced, you will have the tools to choose an attorney who will work to mitigate the costs. You will also have some insight into the emotional versus the legal aspects of divorce. Often the client wastes the most money attempting to resolve emotional issues in the legal system. If you are able to recognize yourself mixing the two, you will save a tremendous amount of money on the divorce.

When an attorney is practicing appropriately, every decision in the process should be weighed on a cost benefit analysis. For example, you are asking the court for X, you may get it or you may get a range from V – Y. It is going to cost you in attorneys' fees approximately _____. From there, you make the decision just like any other financial decision. Is it worth it? The tools of this book are designed to help you pick the kind of attorney who will talk to you in this way. Yes, you may (and often do) choose the path in which the attorney makes the least amount of money. However, that is okay with us. We would rather make $10,000 on five clients who leave happy and satisfied with the process than one client who left more miserable than when they started because they expected the system to do things the system is not designed to do. Now, let me do this same analysis for you. If you save twenty minutes of attorney time as a result of something you read in this book, then the book has paid for itself. The greater likelihood is that you will save thousands of dollars and be happier with the result at the end of the process. Therefore, *Divorce with Joy* is a good investment.

"My brothers and sisters,
whenever you face trials of any kind,
consider it nothing but joy."

—James 1:2 NRS Bible

DIVORCE WITH JOY - THE CONCEPT

Cultivation of Faith - The Beginning

SEPTEMBER 24, 2010 was the day I separated from my Husband. It had been a long time coming but was still unexpected. I made a commitment to him and intended to stay with him for the rest of my life. When I said for better or worse I meant it. Unfortunately, it had really been mostly worse, not a lot of better. Nevertheless, I couldn't wrap my heart around leaving him. It felt selfish. I had been through many divorces as a child. My parents divorced when I was five. My parents then married others and divorced several times over. I just couldn't imagine doing that to my children. For all my Husband's faults, I thought I knew two things about him: 1. He would be a good Father. 2. He would never cheat on me. As it turns out, only one of those was true. So, I found myself in a true emotional crisis. I was ridden with guilt. I have two children. They were five and two at the time. These were exactly the ages my sister and I were when my parents divorced. I went through all the stages of grief starting with anger. I spent much of my time trying to figure out the next right move. I always was a control freak. It is a side effect of being an attorney. Quite literally, you have a person's life in your hands. So, when faced with my own potential divorce, I thought I needed to plan all the contingencies, figure out how to make it work, figure out how to get out, basically figure it out. I was driving myself insane. I was in a constant state of stress. It was horrible. Then the most amazing thing happened.

I picked my son up from his public school one day and he handed me a note. He said, "Mommy, I need to give this to you." I didn't look at it at the time. I just put it in my jacket pocket. Then, I forgot about the note. I was, after all, a thinly veiled mess at this time. A day or so later, I dropped the boys off at school and decided to go for a walk. I was feeling particularly crazy. I didn't know what to do about my marriage, and I hated not knowing where my life was going. I had planned my whole life, graduated high school early, raced through college graduating at age twenty, went directly to law school and was practicing law by twenty-four. As long as I was moving forward, I didn't have to be still. (Yogis will understand that more than most.) But, for the first time in my life, I didn't know where to go next. It was driving me bananas. I thought and rationalized and thought and cried and reasoned and thought. It was never-ending, a circular process leading to nowhere.

It was in this mental chaos that I stepped out for my walk. I got about ¼ a mile and I started talking to God. Back then, I didn't pray very much. I didn't have a relationship with God and I didn't trust Him with my life. I was feeling so hopeless that I didn't know what else to do. So, I just prayed for some help, some guidance or the "answer". There was a chill in the air and I stuck my hands in my pocket. I felt a piece of paper. It was the piece of paper my son had given me a few days before. I pulled it out, and this is what it said, "Trust God to take care of you." As I burst into tears at such a clear and blatant message I turned it over, "Cast all your anxiety on Him because He cares for you."(1 Peter 5:7) "Will you trust Him to take care of you? Circle Yes or No." Seriously? Who gets notes like this from God? The one thing missing was a pencil to circle my choice. This was that note my son insisted he was supposed to give to me. To this day, I have no idea where he got it. I heard the message, finally. For a girl who had never trusted anyone, I learned to trust God. And He has never, ever let me down.

I say all of this to illustrate two points. First, even for me, a divorce is a very emotional process. In law school they don't teach you much substantive law. What they teach you is how to "think like a lawyer". It is basically three years of training and perfecting your logical mind. You learn to be rational, logical and emotionless about the cases presented to you. I worked for nearly a decade assisting people through traumatic circumstances including many, many divorces. I knew the mistakes of others in dealing with divorce because I'd counseled them through it. And yet, here I was struggling with the emotional process. Not one person on Earth is immune. For every single person going through a separation or divorce, it is an emotional process. We all need some guidance through it.

Second, I suggest you pray and trust the process. Whatever you call God, use Him. You will not be able to control this journey you are about to endeavor. You are about to move through an amazing experience, but it is not easy. There is a lot of pain. I had to completely fall apart, challenge my every thought and action and put myself back together into a healthier version of me that is closer to my authentic self. If you end up in a divorce, use the tools in this book to choose an attorney who will act appropriately. You will not be able to control your spouse's behavior. Your spouse will do things you don't like, things that will affect your children. But, you really have to trust the process. Listen to counsel, change within you and your behavior what you can change, and use the tools available to you in the legal process to solve the problems that can be solved. However, know this for sure: The easiest way to get through the process with any semblance of sanity is to let go and let God. This does not require any action whatsoever. It only requires a shift in your heart. From this shift in your heart, comes a shift in your perspective. From this shift in your perspective, comes a shift in your action. I cannot give you a "to do" list of things to accomplish to make this shift in your heart. In *Divorce with Joy* I tell you how it worked for me.

I wouldn't be a good lawyer if I didn't have a disclaimer. My disclaimer: I am not a psychologist, therapist or expert on raising children. I do, however, have a lifetime of unique experiences that have created a passion for encouraging families to think differently about the divorce process. I wish to share with you my experience. I am divorced. I have witnessed people going through a divorce make many mistakes, and I have witnessed really good choices. I have experienced divorce attorneys who helped each of their clients through the process in a healthy and productive way and attorneys who put their own financial gain above the best interest of the client. I have an ability to connect with people, to see their true motivations, and steer them in a better direction. This is why I have been successful in the practice of law. And I have Faith. I happen to believe in the God of Christianity but have no judgment on any other person's belief system. Ultimately, I think God doesn't care what you call Him (or Her for that matter). I believe that God guides our lives, leads us through experiences, so that we may do our part for the greater good.

Do not, however, be turned off by the mention of God and faith as part of the process. My process has led me to a closer relationship with God as I know Him. Your process may do the same; it may not. Either is okay. I only share with you how it worked for me. No two people will have the same experience. Nevertheless, the tools are the same. Therefore, I hope you take from my experience tools that work well in your life and leave the ones that don't quite fit or adapt them to address your specific needs. This book is the story of the places I have been, and I commit my professional and personal experiences to this writing in hopes that it will help. I hope that it is for the greater good. For those who desire to choose better, I want my experiences as expressed through *Divorce with Joy* to help you choose a better way for yourself and your family.

Can I save my marriage?

I remember being there. You find your life in complete shambles. You made a promise before God and your family. You have shared beautiful, wonderful moments with your spouse. Your mind is reeling between unspeakable anger and the depths of loneliness and despair. You wonder, is this the end? Can my marriage be saved?

To prevent confusion, let me start by saying this book is not exactly a guide to saving your marriage. Your happy ever after may include saving this marriage or it may be that you save your family through the divorce process. Saving your marriage and saving your family are completely separate concepts. From here forward you have one of four options: 1. You can stay married, live in dysfunction and chaos and destroy your family. 2. You can stay in the marriage, make it functional and happy and save both your marriage and your family. 3. You can dissolve your marriage, continue the dysfunction and anger of the marriage into the divorce process, giving it greater life and power, and thereby totally destroy your family. 4. You can move forward with divorce, learn to act from a place of love, for yourself and your children, and save your family.

I can tell you that when I took that walk that day, I had no idea where I would end up. Just the thought of divorce burdened me with a heavy weight of guilt and shame. I believed that if I were to divorce my Husband, I would be destroying my family. God helped show me a way to save our family. Our family unit is healthier and happier now than it ever was during the marriage. But, in the early stages, I didn't even realize this was possible. At this point, you don't have to know whether divorce is the right option for you. It is okay to be confused. I was as confused as I ever have been in my life. I just started the work without preconceived notions as to where it would take me. I encourage you to do the same.

Know that I am not a proponent of divorce. (Ironic, I know, coming from a divorce attorney.) I hope that the reader of this book makes every effort to save the family and the marriage. I hope this books helps you to see that, maybe, jumping into divorce is not the best idea. Perhaps it is time to withdraw from conflict and do some work on you. No matter what happened in the marriage, you participated either actively or passively. In order to save your family, you will have to see your role clearly and realize how you participated in the marriage's breakdown. Once you have this insight, it may be possible to save the marriage. Understand that if your family is to be saved, in a marriage or in a divorce, the path forward from this point is exactly the same. Either way it starts right here, with you – with your thought process, with your actions, with your perspective.

People often view divorce as the break-up of a family. This view, in my opinion, is incorrect. While the tenets of this book work whether a divorcing couple has kids or not, the true purpose is to help people who are contemplating divorce learn to navigate the process in a way that serves their children and saves their family. This concept is not really new. Family Law has been geared toward working "in the best interests of the children" for quite some time now. In a divorce, a Judge has broad authority to act in the best interests of the children. Unfortunately, parents often have a difficult time seeing beyond their own emotions and truly doing what is best for their children. Our families need parents who are heroes, especially when going through a divorce or separation. Children and parents will be a family forever. It doesn't end when children turn 18, for in adulthood come graduations, marriages, grandchildren, etc.

You have two choices for your family: 1. Make it functional, whether or not you are married or 2. Allow it to be dysfunctional to the detriment of your children. The choice is that simple. If you believe differently, you are unnecessarily complicating the situation. Children deserve parents who make the hard choices. Children deserve parents who love them more than they hate their spouse. Children deserve parents who do not respond to conflict like 4-year-olds. Children deserve parents who live in love.

Simply because you are contemplating divorce does not mean the love has to be turned off. It should evolve. We should give the spouse the benefit of the doubt and everything done through a separation or divorce should be out of love; love for yourself, love for your children and love (although a different kind of love) for the other parent. I believe we are compelled to love one another, to love every person. The other parent is not exempt from this. As people, we should measure the worth of each act we do each day, both big and small, by the amount of love driving it. A separation and divorce should not be any different.

People become very uncomfortable when I start talking about how they should still love their spouse. The traditional thought is that it is much easier to go through a divorce if you hate or are angry at your spouse. This could not be further from the truth. The only real way to get through the process, from separation forward, is in love. The challenge is to move beyond hate, anger, blame and hurt. In making each choice, including the choice of attorney, ask yourself if you are making this choice from a place of love. This does not mean there won't be conflict. Conflict and love are not mutually exclusive. Conflict is best resolved in love. Out of love comes rationality, logic and, eventually, peace. I believe my clients are most happy with the process when they are able to acquire and implement the tools to divorce in love. Out of love the legal system can work most efficiently.

Why are traditional divorces so hard?

Resistance. People create resistance because they don't know what to do with the love they still have for their spouse. People resist because they don't know what to do with themselves. They have been fighting with their spouses for so long that inertia tells them to keep that up, to continue interacting in the way they always have. Divorces are so hard because people resist change and give energy to the fight instead of giving energy to the healing.

Divorce rates are so high because people do not like to stop and deal with their own issues. They continue to replay the same scenario over and over with the same results - heartache and pain. They think the problems in the marriage are the other person's fault so they get divorced and move on to another relationship. In the new relationship, they find the same old heartache and hurt and they get divorced again. They never stop to evaluate the common denominator in all of their failed marriages. So, as you contemplate divorce, it is time to pause and do some self-evaluation. It is time to find a place from which you can live in love and act based on logic and rationality in place of hurt, anger, confusion, and despair. From that place, a person can make good decisions about the future. The process can be happy and productive and can actually save the family.

You may ask, "How can I go through a divorce in love?" I ask, "How can you not?" You have created beautiful, awesome, wonderful human beings together who came into this world the essence of love and grace. How can you ever not love the person with whom you created such perfect beings? People resist this basic truth and that is a major factor in why divorces are so hard. You will and should always love the Father or Mother of your children. Love is energy; once created, it can never be destroyed. It will evolve and morph into different forms, it may become a different type of love, or it may even become anger, but it is never destroyed.

You may never be able to live in one house as a family but you will always live in the love that created those beautiful souls. It is for them that you focus on healing in place of anger and fear. You are afraid. You're afraid you can't live alone. You're afraid your children will hurt. You're afraid of making the wrong choice. Maybe you're afraid you'll end up with happiness you think you don't deserve. Whatever the fear, don't give energy to it. Give energy to the process of resolving conflict in love. I encourage you to let go of the idea that you have figured anything out. Is divorce the right path for you? Maybe. Can this marriage be saved? Maybe. The only thing that is absolute right now is your commitment to your family, in whatever shape it may ultimately take. Your family will be healthy. Your family will live in love. That is all you know for sure. From there, let's get to work.

Can this process be drama free?

Yes! I talk often about how things are defined by their opposites. Therefore, I am going to attempt to define a "divorce with
joy" by its polar opposite, a "divorce in drama." When I talk about
a drama free divorce, the most common reaction is "That's impossible." I am here to tell you it is not. Drama is the mind's attempt to
create distraction from healing. A separation and potential divorce is
a perfect recipe for the mind to do just that, create distraction from
the healing. A divorce on the Drama Train is one where we focus on
the spouse instead of ourselves. It is one where we attempt to control
the spouse's actions, the timing, the Judge and all the external variables that have an effect on our lives.

In a drama-filled divorce, we are focusing on our pain, the
transgressions against us and the quest for what is "right". We are
focusing on our version of justice. In a drama-filled divorce, we are
lashing out at the spouse in anger and hurt. We are going and going
and going. We are thinking that, if we do or say just the right thing,
we can manipulate the divorce to get exactly what we want. On the
Drama Train, we constantly try to convince people, including our
spouse, we are "right". We have been hurt and we seek to have others
validate our pain. On the Drama Train, we hide from our feelings
and we numb ourselves with our particular addictions. We believe we
cannot love our spouses and divorce them. In a drama filled divorce,
we are motivated primarily by fear and, so, we fight. We take no
time for ourselves and we refuse to see how we contributed to our
current circumstance. On the Drama Train, we all see ourselves as
victims. We have no power to protect or save our families because we
are so engrossed in a fight that we cannot connect with our children.
We are attempting to control things that are beyond our control.
The Drama Train transports us directly to crazy.

How, then, do we experience the conflict that is inevitable
through this process without drama? There is no rule in life that says

when people disagree there necessarily must be drama. Conflict is a test of faith. The way you enter into conflict can greatly determine the way the conflict will be decided. The best way to enter conflict is in joy. Be happy and at peace because your faith is about to be tested. What do you believe? Do you believe this is the worst thing that will ever happen to you? That it's the end of your life? Do you believe that you will be brought through this better or worse? Know that whatever you believe will be. Your life is a reflection of who you think you are. If you believe this is the end of your life, that this will break your family, that you will never be happy again, then you are right. But, if you can hold on in faith to the belief that you and your family will ultimately be okay, that at the end of the journey you will thrive, and that you are not forever relegated to a broken family, then you are right. It is not necessary, at this point, to see how that will happen, just that you have an unfailing belief that it will.

Faith, by definition, is a belief not based on proof. Naturally, past behavior does not lead you to believe that either you or your spouse can emerge from the process happier and healthier people. You have each hurt and been hurt. In the midst of a tumultuous marriage, you tend to see only the hurt and you can't imagine how it ever was or ever will be different. If the two of you communicated and resolved conflict well, you probably wouldn't be contemplating divorce. However, our past does not our future hold. Your past relationship with your spouse is just history. You are entering a time of transition and you can choose, today, how you want to move forward in that relationship with your spouse and your kids. There will be conflict. This conflict is a great opportunity to learn a new way of dealing with your spouse. It should not be wasted by handling it poorly. It should not be wasted by giving in to drama.

You must eliminate the idea that conflict and fighting is always the same thing. A fight is a conflict but a conflict doesn't necessarily have to be a fight. Understand that no matter how much you attempt to shield your children from the fight, there will be fallout. Imagine you and your spouse are in a boxing ring. Each time you throw a punch at your spouse you are also landing that punch on your child. Every black eye you give your spouse you also give your child. Every cut and slash into your spouse also wounds your child. Return to this mental image every time you feel the desire to resolve conflict through fighting. It is almost always not worth it.

The metaphor is in no way an exaggeration. Every bad word or deed directed toward the spouse is absorbed by the children. The question then becomes, "What is the alternative? If I do not fight through a conflict, how do I handle conflict?" The answer? Don't fight. Stand in stillness. Know that when you are fighting, it is impossible to listen. You can't hear your children. You can't be sensitive to their needs and you can't truly interact with them. Fighting through a conflict consumes all of your mental and emotional space and becomes, whether you intend so or not, your singular focus. You don't have to back down. You don't have to cower away; just stand firm. Instead of showering your kids with the fallout of a war, shower you kids with the love that overflows from a change in your heart and thoughts and from resolving your conflict with your spouse from a healthy, productive place. It is, ultimately, the greatest example for your children.

How do I get my happy ever after?

There are three basic components which facilitate your happy ever after: 1. Cultivating Faith 2. Working on Self and 3. Moving Forward. The order is intentional. Traditionally, people skip right over one and two and go directly to "I'm divorcing that S.O.B." We will talk in this book about times when you may have to move forward before you are well founded in the initial phases, but those times are the exception and not the rule. I am going to let you in on a little secret. Most of this book isn't about divorce. Only at the end, once you have moved to a place where you see with clarity that divorce is the right option for you, do we really talk about divorce.

If you are recently separated from your spouse, you are probably not in a place to decide to save the marriage or get divorced. As a result, the vast majority of the work we do through the book and the work I encountered on my path had nothing to do with the legal process of divorce. It was all about me and this will be all about you. Understand that this is a vital part of the process. It is the foundation for a life moving forward that is healthy and happy, married or single. If divorce is the ultimate outcome, the divorce process is then functional, drama free and therapeutic. With this foundation, if a divorce is the ultimate outcome, your family is better for it. The result is not a broken home but two healthy, happy homes in which children thrive.

The Foundation

My Husband moved out of the house on that day in September. My first step was to disengage from him. My marriage was broken-that was for sure. A marriage only has two components, Husband and Wife. Two halves make the whole. If the marriage was broken and dysfunctional, then so was I. It was time to repair my half. However, I couldn't do that while I was actively participating in the dysfunction of the marriage. So, my first step was to shift focus. I had to put my Husband in a box and lock him away for a time. (Metaphorically speaking of course.)

I am giving you fair warning that this is hard. It is hard to admit all of your faults and shortcomings and work to change them. Your disease, addiction, or ill thinking that drove you to this place is a powerful force. It will tell you there is no other way. It will breed doubt, hopelessness and negativity. When these thoughts come in (and they will for everyone) have faith. Keep your eye on the prize of a happy family at the end of the process. I am here to tell you that it can happen.

Both professionally and personally, I have seen it play out time and again. People become fixated on their spouse and refuse to stop and look in the mirror. I admit to doing this for a time myself. It is too easy to point out all the things your spouse did wrong, all the things he needs to change. It is also pointless because YOU can't change those things. You can only change and control you. It is time to shift the focus away from the finger pointing cattiness and shift focus inward towards a strength that can only be achieved through self-reflection and self-change.

This separation is about fighting for your kids not fighting with your spouse. Almost everyone contemplating a divorce comes to me thinking that the fighting with their spouse is the source of the problem. Fighting with your spouse is not the root of all the evil your marriage has become. It is a symptom, a distraction from the real problems, an outlet for feelings a person has yet to process. The real issue in my marriage was me. The real issue in your marriage is you.

WORKING ON SELF
The Genesis

I Love My Children Enough to Fix Myself

IT will take time for you to forgive and continue to love your spouse in a way that is healthier than during the marriage. Don't be frustrated because you are not there yet. More importantly, don't allow your spouse or your feelings about her to be your focus. Step two is about finding your place of peace from which you can make logical, rational decisions. A Divorce with Joy begins with cultivating an unfailing belief that you and your family will thrive at the end of the process. It then moves into an effort to learn to live in love. If you find your marriage on the rocks, chances are you haven't lived in love for a long time. Perhaps you never truly did. It is time to learn to live in love and happiness and it starts with loving yourself. You must fully utilize this time of transition and evolve as a person into a better, healthier individual. For me, the mantra that drove this process was, "I love my children enough to fix myself."

There are two concepts behind this mantra you must understand.

1. It is easy to stay wrapped up in the same old fight you have had with your spouse for 10 years. You still have feelings for your spouse. Maybe you want to fight with him just so you have contact. Or maybe you want to fight with him to remind yourself of the reasons you are getting divorced in the first place. You fight to counteract the love you still

feel but don't know how to process. All of those things are normal. Recognize when you are doing them and stop, for the sake of your children, just stop.

Your spouse will likely want to continue fighting for the same reasons. Do not engage. Let your spouse have his own process. Understand it has nothing to do with you and your process. If you stop engaging, eventually there will be no payoff to your spouse for this behavior. How much fun is it, after all, to realize you are all alone in a fight? At that point, your spouse will have to stop the behavior and figure out a different way of relating to you. People have a hard time continuing to be angry in the face of grace. Continue to give your spouse grace and the greatest likelihood is that he will eventually come around. If he doesn't, then at least you have become happier and healthier in the process. But, if you never get out of the cycle of fighting, neither you nor your children will ever find happiness. So the genesis of learning to live in love is to step out of the life you have been living, disengage from your spouse, and work on "fixing" you.

2. If you don't fix you, you will pass on your issues to your children. If you give an honest evaluation of yourself, you will probably find that most of your issues started a long time ago, most likely in childhood. Your children are going to emulate one or the other of the parents in their adult relationships. Imagine your child is in the very same situation as an adult. Would you want them to behave the way that you are behaving? Is the life you have right now good enough for your child? For me, the answer was a resounding "NO!" My children deserve better than to be miserable, confused, angry and in turmoil. I love my kids enough to fix me so they can have a better life.

Childhood Origins

Please believe me when I tell you that I don't really want to tell you all the intimate and gory details of my process any more than you want to face the intimate and gory details of your own. But, you find yourself in a relationship that isn't working any longer. I have interviewed hundreds and hundreds (maybe even thousands) of people who found themselves in the same position. I can promise you that, within a few questions, it was pretty easy to see how the dysfunction in their marriage was rooted in childhood.

We have an amazing ability to deceive ourselves. We will tell you our lives today have nothing to do with our childhood, that we are nothing like our parents and that all of that childhood stuff is psycho-babble nonsense. I probably would have said the same thing before I started this process. Nevertheless, here is what I discovered.

This part of the book makes me the most uncomfortable. I was taught shame as a toddler. I was taught to keep secrets, to not trust my instincts and to believe that things were acceptable that clearly were not. I was taught that if people knew the whole truth about me they wouldn't love me or accept me. So, I struggled with great anxiety about telling my story. I am afraid people will judge me, reject me or think that I am crazy. I am afraid the people I love will be disappointed or hurt by exposing the past. I hope that every person reading this book knows I have only the best intentions in telling my story, even if my truth paints some people in a light they view as unfavorable.

I worked tirelessly to find a way to write a book that conveyed the ideas I need to convey without exposing my whole life to the world. Ultimately, I couldn't find a way. The mature, intellectual part of me knows you need to know the whole truth. I imagine if you didn't know exactly what I was going through, you might say, "Oh well that's easy for her to say. She had it good. She is an attorney. She couldn't possibly know what I am experiencing." Believe me when I tell you that separating from my Husband wasn't easy for me. I was dealing with a lifetime of pain. I'd learned to cope with that pain in a certain way. However, the way that I'd coped was not healthy for me or my children. My marriage was only a symptom of that dysfunction. It was an external reflection of my internal chaos, a distraction from the issues I needed to face.

Knowing that it is necessary to tell my story as it happened doesn't change the fact that part of me is very afraid to lay it all out for public consumption. But, here is the thing: It is a terrifying journey you are about to begin. It takes a tremendous amount of bravery. The easy, self-indulgent path is to continue to wallow in misery, fight with your spouse and refuse to take an accounting of your faults, problems, sickness and issues. It is hard to "fix" yourself and ultimately only you can do it. However, if you want to come out of this process a happier and healthier person, a stronger family unit, it is absolutely necessary. So I tell my story so that you know you are not alone. No matter how bad the past, the future can be better. I am not special. I am not stronger than you. I am a regular person with faults and cracks that are just as beautifully messed up as yours. You can do this and it will be worth it.

I met my Husband when I was 21 years old. I was in law school at the time. He was really my first relationship. I'd been the queen of attracting bad guys. Without divulging too many details, trust me on this one. If he was an emotionally unavailable loser with no intention of having a relationship, he was the one I managed to snag. From nice guys who were locked in the back of the proverbial "closet"; to married guys claiming to be single; to sex, drug and alcohol addicts, they were the ones I gravitated towards. I see now I was attracting them on purpose. I was reinforcing my belief that I didn't deserve love. It is a fact that I didn't know how to function in relationships. It is taking years for me to uncover all of the subconscious beliefs that drive my actions. Frankly, I'm still working on that one.

Over the course of my lifetime, I'd sought many outlets to stifle my pain, including drugs, alcohol, food, work, school, success, exercise, men, vacations, and the list goes on and on. I didn't see any of this when I first separated. I thought I'd just found myself in a "bad" marriage and I needed to fix the marriage or get divorced. By "fixing" the marriage, I really thought I just needed to "fix" my Husband. After all, he was the alcoholic who had cheated on me. How could the break-up of the marriage be my fault? Oh my. Our ability to self-deceive!

The Lessons of Children

I was 26 when I got married and pregnant. I was 27 when our first son was born. Our first son taught me true feeling. It struck me that I was responsible for this beautiful, innocent soul who came here unscathed, pure and perfect. There is something very profound about the first few minutes of life. It is the closest we will ever be to God. I learned, in the instant of his birth, what it meant to love. I had never loved or known love before he was born. I'd never loved myself, but I loved him. And, I'd do anything in the world to keep him as pure, innocent and unscathed as possible. That moment shared with my Husband and our new son was one of the most profound and beautiful of my entire life. Anytime I find myself wanting to backslide and lash out at the Father of my children, I take myself back to that moment. It is, I believe, the truest picture of who we are as people, the closest we ever were to our authentic selves with one another. It is a helpful image when choosing to live with grace in our relationship.

In moments of sobriety, my Husband was a very good and loving Father. He connected with our son and was an involved parent who changed diapers and gave bottles. We were able to ignore the problems of our marriage by focusing very intently on the demands of being first time parents. I walked around with a significant amount of anxiety. I was vulnerable to this child that I loved so much. I would lie in bed many nights worrying about the millions of ways he could get hurt, physically, mentally or emotionally. I'd never really experienced vulnerability like that before having children. I had always raced and raced to accomplish goals, with little regard for feelings or emotions. As a result, I'd never had any relationship that I was afraid to lose. I'd built a fortress around myself for protection that was, until my son was born, impenetrable.

I realized, even then, that my life was not good enough for my son. I had no idea, however, how to change it. When our son was about two, we began to come out of our new parent stupor. We didn't want our son to be an only child. I sort of had an instinct that he would need a sibling before all of this was over. We wanted him to know the unconditional love of a person other than his parents. We wanted him to have a true partner in life. So, I got pregnant again.

Our second son came here the spitting image of me. He was a very happy, if challenging, baby. He giggled and was playful. I understand it is somewhat odd to describe a baby or toddler as charismatic, but he has always been extremely charismatic. He was born with a zest for life. I recognized that I came here the same way. Wow, had I gotten off track. I did not walk around with the same (pardon the word) joy. As I watched our son explore the world, I admired his spirit. Watching him gave me a glimpse into my authentic self. I vowed that I would get back to that person, the happy one, the one that loved life. I would take back my Joy. And so the process began.

The Root of My Problems

There was an event that occurred very early in my life that I didn't consciously remember. However, this event had driven every aspect of my entire life. I'd always shown the symptoms of a person who'd been the victim of sexual abuse- the promiscuity, the inability to connect to the opposite sex, the emotional eating, etc. However,

I didn't have any memories of sexual abuse. The memories came, for the first time, when I separated from my Husband. I have since learned that it is not all that unusual for a person to have memories of sexual abuse for the first time during a traumatic experience like a divorce.

Prior to the conscious memories, I could never relax. I was always full of anxiety. I would walk around with physical symptoms like pressure in my chest and irritable bowel syndrome. Without a doubt, I have never felt as emotionally unstable as when these memories began to surface. I did not want to deal with any of it. I wanted to curl up and sleep until the world was right again. It was a very dark endeavor to go back and relive the abuse and put it in the rightful place. I didn't feel up to the task. I had serious doubts as to whether I could live through the abuse and the divorce at the same time. I had urges to fight with my Husband because at least that was pain I could manage. I loved my children enough to resist those urges most of the time.

This period was the hardest, darkest time in my life. Ultimately, though, there was no other choice. I had to break everything down and dig out the core of all the issues that led me to this place in life. I had to pick myself up and face it, not because I wanted to or because it was easy or because it felt good, but because my boys deserved for me to be the best parent I could be. All of this and the persona that I'd developed to cope with such immense childhood trauma had to be disassembled. The "me" that I'd known my whole life was not really me at all. She had to fall apart to be put back together again. To say that it was difficult is to say that the Grand Canyon is a small hole in the ground.

My entire life had been a distraction from this basic truth. I was molested at a very young age, and I'd spent my life running from the pain that act caused. I struggled with believing that my mind could hide this from me for so long. I felt crazy dealing with the memories and the separation from my Husband all at once. I see now that, had I remembered the abuse earlier in life, I probably would have ended up in an asylum. I could barely process it in my 30s. I am not sure I could have processed it as a child. And, as long as I was in a dysfunctional marriage, I couldn't deal with it either. It was only once I removed myself from the day-to-day relationship with my Husband and created an emotionally safe place for me, that I could begin to remember, and eventually heal, this pain. My psyche had deceived itself my entire life as an act of self-preservation and, in that sense, it had worked. In many ways, I functioned well in society. But, behind all of my success, I was a mess. It was affecting my relationship with me, my children, my Husband, and God. When I disengaged from everything that I had been using to distract me from the real issue, the healing could begin. It did, however, get worse before it got better.

The Break Down

As I began to get to the core, I encountered what I affectionately call a breakdown. I found myself in a precarious mental and emotional state. My breakdown was the most productive and therapeutic occurrence of my entire life. It has no negative connotation whatsoever. Literally, I did break down. I broke down everything I thought about my relationship with my spouse. I broke down everything I thought about my relationship with myself. I broke down my perspective, world view and spirituality. Essentially, I broke down my whole world. Don't be afraid of the breakdown. From the rubble, comes new life.

Fear is the natural reaction of our psyche when faced with real and lasting change. The person who will emerge at the end of the process is unknown. The unknown is terrifying. But, is it any more terrifying than living the remaining years of your life in the same patterns and dysfunction? Is it any scarier than damaging your children because you were too afraid to do the hard work? For me, the answer was no. It was scary, but so was the thought of things never getting better. So, I recognized that as I "broke down" I might need some external touchstones to sanity, also known as the shared reality. Consequently, I created a "Board of Directors," a group of trusted advisors who helped me grow and maintain perspective throughout the process. Here's how the recipe worked for me:

BOARD OF DIRECTORS
Therapist,
Friend,
Trainer/Nutritionist,
Spiritual Advisor,
Business/Life Coach

Therapy

The role of therapy is vital to the process. Separating from your spouse is an extremely emotional process. It is a time of transition, and when used properly can be the catalyst for real, life-improving change. If handled improperly it can be just the opposite. It can send you into a downward spiral from which it is hard to recover. Therapy can be the deciding factor in whether the change will be positive or negative.

You will have emotions and growing pains as you adjust from an intact marriage to a separated couple. You are in the process of learning new ways of dealing with your spouse. The process works much more efficiently if there is a third party perspective to help guide you along the path. The extent to which you do the work of therapy will greatly determine how well or how poorly the separation (and divorce if you eventually get there) process goes. Therapy is the first step. Therapy should be sought prior to an attorney (unless, of course, there is an emergency situation), prior to filing divorce, and prior to making any big life changes.

People do not make wise decisions when they are overcome with emotions. You should never make the decision to divorce from a place of anger, hate or hurt. The fact is that broken people yield broken children. No matter how difficult you find the concept of self-reflection and self-improvement, you must commit to the process. It is the foundation for a life lived in love and a divorce process that saves the family. Therapy, however, has many facets and dimensions. For me, it began with four major components: Escape, Reaching Out, Meditation and Therapeutic Counseling.

ESCAPE. Escape is quite intentionally first on the list. In the very beginning, I had thoughts and emotions that I just could not handle. It is generally not considered a positive thing to escape from life's problems. However, in the beginning, I had no choice. I was not equipped with the tools to deal with the things happening in my life. For me, the greatest escape was wine. I don't advocate the abuse of alcohol in any way. I can now admit that alcohol was on the list of my addictions. My definition of addiction is any act or substance which you use to escape reality or delay processing emotions. Wine wasn't a severe addiction, but I did escape using alcohol. I used alcohol to cope with feelings that I didn't have the strength or mental fortitude to deal with at the time. That, by my definition, makes it an addiction.

You will not be able to get through a Divorce with Joy abusing alcohol, drugs, food, sex or any other substance. However, I can tell you that, in the very early stages, a bottle of wine at night after the boys went to bed was helpful. (Notice I said bottle, not glass.) I felt so lonely, desperate, sad, hopeless and helpless that I needed to escape into a bottle of wine. As I continued to heal, I found I needed this escape less and less. Your therapeutic counselor will tell you not to escape into alcohol. That is sound advice. I say, be nice to your-self. Do what you have to do to get through these initial stages. Just keep focused on your kids. Don't become so self-indulgent that you do anything that jeopardizes the safety or welfare of your children. Never, ever drunk text, call or email your spouse or anyone other than your trusted friend on your Board of Directors. Obviously, don't use alcohol if you have a history of alcoholism. If you ever once break these rules, cut yourself off from the use of alcohol and find a healthier momentary reprieve. People use many alternatives to escape including television, internet, drama, sports, competitive games, painting, etc. The list is as long and unique as our personalities. Whatever your escape, take the necessary steps in the early stages to keep going.

REACH OUT. You will need to build a support system in order to get through this process. This is a group of friends who will listen to you vent for free (as opposed to paying a therapeutic counselor to listen to you vent). Your work with a counselor should be very directional and working towards goals. You don't want to pay a therapist just to listen to you gripe about how your Wife or Husband is a jerk. Nevertheless, you need to get these feelings off your chest. It is important that you have a person or group of people who will simply listen.

When picking friends for your Board of Directors, be mindful that they are the type of friends who will actually help the situation. If your marriage is a mess, it stands to reason that many of your friendships may be a mess too. We all have those friends who are gossips, those who thrive on hearing how bad your life is and love to keep drama going. This is not who you should pick for your Board of Directors. It may be tempting because on some level this friend will make you feel better. This friend will share your anger and talk poorly about your spouse and vindicate your animosity. That is precisely why you should not be discussing anything with this friend.

The purpose of a friend or group of friends on your Board of Directors is not to have a spouse bashing contest. Keep in mind you may decide in the end you want to attempt to save your marriage. If you have spilled your guts to the drama fiend friend, he or she will use that information later on to stir up more drama.

Now, if you have been in a drama-filled marriage, you may not be in a close relationship with someone suitable for your Board of Directors. If you have been the drama queen or king, the "normal" friends who are emotionally stable and adverse to drama probably put you in a box so that you didn't drive them crazy. It's not that the person is no longer a friend, but the person probably only tolerates you in small doses because you carry too much drama. You may want to contact this person and rekindle a friendship. If you are venting with a purpose (that purpose being to process feelings as opposed to wallowing in misery) then your stable friend won't mind listening. And, you can trust this friend not to get too wrapped up in your problems, to maintain perspective, and to point out when you are going overboard or are being unproductive.

Also, there should be at least one friend on your Board of Directors who can see things from your spouse's point of view. You won't always want to hear it. And you may strongly disagree. But you have to be able to see both sides if you are going to properly heal through the process. I suggest discussing with this friend his role on your Board and openly give him permission to tell you the other (i.e. your spouse's) side of the issue. Then don't get mad when the person fulfills your request. After all, it is for the greater good.

I found it difficult to reach out to friends. I'd never really talked much about the reality of my marriage. I protected him a lot. In the same way that I didn't want people to know the true me because I thought they wouldn't love me, I didn't want people to know the true him because I thought they wouldn't love him. I learned to let go of that. I had a few very good friends who would listen without judgment and lend support and guidance. When I wanted to fight with my Husband, I vented to a friend instead. When I had a sense that maybe I was having an irrational reaction to something, I expressed whatever I was feeling (no matter how crazy it sounded, even to me) to a friend. It just helped to say things out loud. Those things we keep bottled up tend to fester and grow. It would not have helped to say those things to my Husband. It would've just started an argument.

So use your Board of Directors as your outlet. They can help you process feelings and let them go. They can help you maintain perspective and stay in touch with reality. When I reached the point that I was able to forgive my Husband, my friends didn't say, "Remember what a jerk you said he was just the other day?" They had total amnesia for everything I ever said from a place of hurt, anger or frustration. And the beautiful thing is that, at some point, so did I.

JOURNALING. In the course of my separation, I began to keep a journal. Initially, it wasn't a log of events or a recording of history so much as an expression of thoughts and feelings. Early on in the process, it was difficult to identify what I was feeling. It seemed like I was caught up in a current of emotions that were swirling around me and merging together. I wasn't able to identify any one emotion in particular. Therefore, it helped to sit down and write. Often my journal was free flowing thoughts and feelings. It didn't follow any logical order and wouldn't make sense to anyone reading it. However, it was helpful to get those things out of my head and on paper. Then I could begin to categorize and understand what was happening on the inside.

As I progressed, my writing evolved into a more traditional journal. It helped to write down what was going on in my life so that I could deal with emotions independently and not rely so heavily on my Board of Directors. However, the best thing about the journal is the perspective it provides on your progress. Sometimes when I get discouraged I go back and read last year's journal. I amaze myself at the progress I have made. When we are truly healing, our minds have an amazing ability to forget the pain of the past. When I review my journal I am filled with immense gratitude for how far I have come in the process. I can see how much better my life is now than it was when I first wrote in the journal. The perspective is invaluable.

If for no other reason, journaling is worth the effort so that you can keep a record of your progress and practice gratitude for the things you have accomplished, even if there is still hard work ahead.

MEDITATIVE PRACTICE. Sometimes the best way forward is to be still. We don't always know the answer going forward. If you are "struggling" for the next right step, it means there shouldn't be a next step. You have to learn to just be still. It is hard because when we are afraid or confused we want to do something. We want to repair the situation. We want to figure things out. Yoga taught me you can't figure anything out. This is a very difficult lesson for a controlling, overbearing, strong-willed personality. Answers aren't achieved, they are revealed after patience and over time. When you can ease into a path moving forward that feels right, you have your answer. Until then, meditate.

The thing about divorce is that when you are in a marriage, it is the foundation of your life. The two of you are building a home and a life together and that is the window from which you see everything. When that marriage is dysfunctional and potentially over, you don't know who you are anymore. Your foundation is rocked. What I discovered is that I never knew me at all. I married young and was absorbed into a couple. I remember my therapist asking me once (and this was before my separation), "What do you like to do?" I was flabbergasted that I had no answer. I had no idea what I liked. None. How do you get to be in your early 30s and have no idea what you like?

Meditation helps you to get to know you. It is easy in this noisy world of television, tabloids, work, kids, spouses, cell phones, Facebook (and on and on) to get caught up in the distractions of the world and lose touch with your essential, authentic self. You must find a way to shut out all of the noise. Now, in the process of separation, is the time to figure out what you want, what you like and what kind of relationship will work for you going forward. Certainly the one you've had hasn't worked. The only way to do this is to be still, be alone, and in that space, become comfortable. Then, you can really learn and listen. You can receive answers and ease into solutions.

In the earlier stages, I often felt defeated and depressed, like I couldn't face the world. By the time I'd put on my game face to get through work, I couldn't muster the energy to get through a killer workout. But, I needed to start transitioning into better ways to manage stress. My transition started with yoga. At first, it was extremely frustrating. I see now that I had so much garbage in the way that I couldn't relax in yoga or any other meditation. The more frustrating meditation is in the beginning, the more you need it. So, I kept going

Learning to function with a calm mind in the face of external and internal chaos is an invaluable tool to help you think clearly and make rational decisions. The stillness will, at first, be extremely uncomfortable. That is okay. Discomfort is a feeling with which you will have to become intimately familiar. Acknowledge the discomfort and discuss it with your advisors. But, keep going until you perfect comfort in the stillness. It will be a helpful tool in the months and years to come. The road may get rockier before it calms.

Find your way. Your way may not be yoga. It could be non-moving meditation, it could be on walks, it could be as you do a repetitive creative practice like crochet or knitting, it could be gardening, it could be hitting golf balls or fishing, it could be just sitting and consciously breathing. It doesn't matter which mechanism you choose so long as it quiets the mind and aligns you with you.

Whatever your method, however, it should be a daily practice. The process you are undertaking develops your essential self and deflates the ego that has developed over your lifetime, often as means of self-protection. Whatever your tool of connecting with the most essential you is perfect. And, by the way, this takes time. You may not have the faintest idea what I'm talking about at this point. It's okay. Just fake it until you make it. Your effort is a beautiful thing.

You'll appreciate it the more you get to know you. Practice patience and love with yourself.

During this time, I also found that it helped to read a daily meditation. Often, our minds are reeling. I found it was helpful to focus on something outside of my own mind and not directly related to the divorce. I used a book published by Hazelden Meditation Series called *The Language of Letting Go* written by Melody Beattie. It was and continues to be very helpful to me. Some people use a Bible study. Some people use a mediation series related to yoga. Really it's whatever works for you. I find that God gives us exactly what we need. If you feel an instinct or a whisper telling you to pick up a certain book, I would say pick up that book. It is probably exactly what you need to hear. But, it is good to get out of your thoughts in meditation and seek a new way of thinking. An effective way to do this is to meditate on the works and thoughts of others. I often find much revelation there.

THERAPEUTIC COUNSELING. As I said, meditation and yoga were so hard for me because I had a mountain of invisible garbage in the way. At the time, I didn't realize this was why it was so hard. I just thought I "couldn't relax." Now, I see why I couldn't relax. It was because I was desperately holding on to a bunch of emotional and mental baggage.

Later in the book, I will talk to some degree about drama vs. abuse. Where you are on the spectrum between drama and abuse will determine the level at which you need to seek counseling. If, for example, you have drama going on, then maybe you can get by with self-help books or a divorce support group. Maybe, if you're somewhere in the middle of the spectrum, counseling through church or another third party who has some training but isn't a licensed therapist would work to get you through the process. However, if you are on the side of the spectrum closer to abuse or severe abuse of any kind, either before or during your marriage, then perhaps a more highly trained, skilled professional is a better fit for you.

The therapist who ultimately worked best for me is highly trained and didn't accept insurance so it was an out-of-pocket expense. Often the most experienced therapists don't accept insurance because it is a hassle. These therapists have a thriving practice without insurance clients because they are effective and experienced. People often don't want to spend that kind of money on counseling but will spend thousands of dollars on a divorce. Trust me; the money spent in therapy is much better utilized.

As I progressed in the separation, I really began some deep cleaning. I was very grateful for the tools I'd developed through meditation and therapy. A common misperception is that the toughest part of the process is the separation from your spouse and the idea of potentially getting divorced. In reality, the toughest part is cleaning out your own internal mess that led you to this place. It is a process of taking your psyche, experiences and world view apart and putting it back together more functional and whole. The process is uncomfortable. Your brain will fight itself. We have lived an unhealthy life because on some level we believed that is what we deserved, and in some ways, it worked for us. It will take time and great effort to train yourself to believe differently and to stop the old patterns of self-sabotage. As a result, it is vital to have a good therapist.

Prior to my separation I'd been seeing a therapist for some time. She was good in her own way, and I am grateful for her. She laid solid foundation for things to come. But she wasn't the right therapist to guide me through the hard work. I liked her and could talk to her like a girlfriend. As I was going through the separation, I attempted to do counseling with my Husband and went to a person who practiced addiction and marriage counseling. I instantly liked him and trusted him. He was, in a sense, my Husband fast forwarded thirty years after a lifetime of recovery. I wanted him to be my individual therapist. As the very wise man he is, he gently guided me in a different direction. I ended up with a female therapist who, in the initial meeting, made me extremely uncomfortable. I literally had to make myself go back to see her. The only reason I did was because I trusted the man who sent me to her.

On some level, I knew she would challenge everything about me and my view of the world. The biggest part of me wanted to run as far away from her as I could get. But, I couldn't accept that for myself. I kept telling myself, "You want better for your boys than this. They deserve a happy, healthy mom. If you don't fix you, you will raise broken children. They are worthy of more." So, I kept going. It was horrible, painful and uncomfortable. Much of the time I walked around feeling as though I couldn't breathe. There was so much coming to the surface in therapy, and I fought an over-whelming instinct to push it back down and keep the scary stuff buried. I was the vessel of an internal war.

During this time, I was a thinly veiled mess. My mind told me this wasn't necessary. I could just deal with the issues of my marriage. I didn't have to deal with this crap. My mind told me one had nothing to do with the other and that my therapist must be a sadist who just likes to see people in pain. My brain told me that I'd done perfectly well without dealing with all of this garbage. After all, I had a career and two beautiful children. My life wasn't that bad. I told myself there was no purpose in going through all the pain my brain had buried for a reason. All of these thoughts are a form of negative self-talk with a huge portion of self-deception. If you have a deep rooted desire for the best for you and your children, you have to clean all that stuff out in therapy. This is true even though it gets worse, sometimes much worse, before it gets better.

When I said earlier it takes great courage to go through the process, this is what I meant. It takes great courage to break down and rebuild. It takes great courage to fall apart. It is much harder than simply getting divorced and moving on. I believe that's why so many people don't do it. They refuse to do the work and just bring their baggage to the next marriage only to find themselves in the same place a few years later. I encourage you to stop now, before you dissolve this marriage, and fix you. Maybe then, you'll find the marriage can be rebuilt. In my case, it was a long process, but my Board of Directors got me through it. I did the best I could to practice self- love throughout. I went to some very dark places and cleaned them out. It is better to live a short time of misery, as you go through the process of cleaning out, than to live a lifetime of misery because you never did the cleaning. Remember that when you want to quit.

ADDICTION. For many people, part of the cleaning out process includes addressing addiction. My opinion is that every person on the planet is addicted to something. Some of us are a lot addicted to a few things. Some of us are a little addicted to a lot of things. Some of us are both. Our lives to date have taught us a coping mechanism for dealing with the icky parts of life. For me, the major addiction is food. (As I continued my path I discovered a few more. We'll discuss those another day.) As a child you don't have many options for a coping mechanism. It isn't as if at three you can go grab a beer, do a line of cocaine, etc. So, my addiction became food. It fit well with my southern upbringing where we are taught from a young age that every sad or happy occasion is celebrated or soothed with food. It gave me the added bonus that if I were severely overweight, I wouldn't have to deal with the sexual advances of men. If I were fat enough, my abuser would leave me alone.

In some ways it worked. I am not sure why he stopped. Maybe it was because he got married and the opportunity wasn't there as much. Maybe it was because I became old enough to talk and tell on him. Maybe it was because I became morbidly obese. At five years old, I weighed 125 pounds and wore a women's size 12 that my Mother would hem at the knees so that they would be long pants for me. I suppose I will never truly know why the abuse stopped. But, I do know that it spawned some truly addictive aspects of my personality. Your addiction may be food, alcohol, sex, drama, self-mutilation, anorexia, nicotine, drugs, pornography or relationships. The list of potential addictions is truly endless. It's time to figure out the nature and extent of your addiction. If you don't, it will keep you from being happy. You will risk spiraling into this addiction instead of dealing with the things you need to confront.

NUTRITIONIST/TRAINER. As you begin to come out of the fog of the initial phases and prepare to move forward, it is important to begin to take care of your body. You have tackled a tremendous task of self-evaluation, self-improvement and cleaning out. As you move further into that process, it is good to begin to implement positive tools to help you move forward. For me, the bridge between the really horrible stuff I had to work on in therapy in the beginning and the really wonderful life that came later was nutrition and exercise.

I encourage you, therefore, to engage the services of a personal trainer and nutritionist. I transitioned into an all organic diet for our family. This helped our children immensely with attention and hyperactivity issues, focus and mood. It also helped me quite a bit. By detoxing my body from all of the processed foods, chemicals, sugars, and so forth, I found that my mood was lighter. I had substantially more energy. This is extremely helpful when transitioning from a partnership to a single parent. When suddenly you find yourself with the added responsibility of doing 100% care for the kids, 80% of the time, the extra energy is a must.

I hear people complain that they don't have enough money to take care of their body properly. These same people smoke cigarettes, spend thousands of dollars on a divorce, spend hundreds of dollars a month on prescriptions and doctors or drive brand new cars. We all have money for those things which we make a priority. One day, as I was pumping gas, I saw a man exit his $80,000 car and purchase a tank full of premium unleaded gas. I thought to myself, "If only he cared as much about his body as he does about his car. When his car stops working he can always buy a new one, he can never buy a new body". I would bet he didn't eat healthy or organic.

His vehicle was clearly a priority. His body did not seem to be on the same level of importance.

I choose to prioritize my body over material possessions. Someone who lives in a place of love respects and cherishes the body cares for it in a way that is worthy of only the best. When you love yourself enough to take care of yourself, the whole world gets better. Your body is the window to the world. If you are sick or tired or feel poorly, your world view will reflect these feelings. If you feel good and are properly fueled, it is much easier to take on the tasks of life with a good attitude and perspective. The benefits of taking care of your body, therefore, reach far beyond looking and feeling good. When you care for yourself, the sky is truly the limit. It is vastly easier to get through the process happy if you feel good physically. Consequently, diet and exercise were a very important piece to my puzzle.

As you proceed through the process of "cleaning out" and addressing any addiction, you will want to start replacing old habits. Of all the addictions you can have, addiction to exercise is a pretty good one. The closer I moved to my authentic self, the more I realized nourishing my body well and engaging in regular exercise is an act of love. We are only given one body and it works most efficiently not as a sedentary object but as a being in motion. The endorphins created by exercise are God's anti-depressant. I get a certain "high" from exercise that was very helpful. Eventually my body became accustomed to the effect exercise has on my mental and physical health, and I miss it if I get out of the habit of exercise. Being active also got me out of the house and back into the world a little bit. For me, it was the first twinkle of the light at the end of the tunnel. I have seen people replace bad habits with all sorts of new, healthier stuff. In my case it was exercise. For you it could be anything that you love that makes you feel well and that helps you to focus on the positive things of life. Find something that breeds gratitude.

LIFE OR RELATIONSHIP COACH. A life or relationship coach is different from a therapeutic counselor. My therapeutic counselor was dealing with the remnants of trauma. After I made progress with my therapist, a coach was useful to take the next steps. I have engaged more than one coach over the years, each for a different purpose. Each coach helped me implement the tools I learned in counseling and develop a specific strategy and plan for moving forward. Coaches were useful for accountability as well. It was helpful to have the perspective of someone on the outside looking in. My coach wasn't there in the beginning and only knew the "me" who had undergone significant healing. Therefore, the coach was effective in helping me get to know the new, more functional me. My coaches helped pull ideas and desires out of me. They helped me figure out what I truly wanted out of life. The further I progressed in healing, the less the existence I'd built prior to therapy seemed to fit. My coaches helped me build the life that I want, the life that was deserving of my healing.

SPIRITUALITY. If exercise and good nutrition were the bridge to the other side, developing a relationship with God was the great reward of the journey. After I did the cleaning out of all the negative stuff that had accumulated in my heart and mind over the course of my life, I was left with an emptiness. It is not a craving or lonely feeling of emptiness, for your life takes on meaning as you clean it up. It is more like a void. I heard a pastor say once that there is a God shaped vacuum in every person's life that can only be filled by the spirit of the Lord. After I did the hard work of the initial phases, this was very much true.

One day on the way to school, we passed a church. My oldest, who was six at the time, said, "Hey Mommy, there is a church. You know where people get married and get buried." Even though the way he expressed this was quite funny, I felt that pang of guilt that my child only knew of church in those two contexts. So, we began attending church regularly. Truly, it was one of the best decisions I ever made. I find my children often lead me in the direction of the truest answers, instead of it being the other way around. How is that for the irony of life?

Through church, I learned not to follow the rules and dogma of religion, but to develop a very personal and loving relationship with God. We may not be able to follow the "rules" churches lay out for us in the beginning. I allowed that to prevent me from attending for a long time. When I developed a personal and loving relationship with God, He helped me decipher what is right for me. Once this happened, I discovered I was following many of the "rules" of the church that I once found so difficult. I found I was more and more comfortable in church and less worried about how the people of the church were judging me. I became confident in my relationship with God and, in that comfort, other people's views about me faded into irrelevance. Often I cried through the services (and still can't hold back tears in the presence of the Holy Spirit). The pastor said, "Every service should be a healing service." The best churches are not those that preach on hell like they want you to go there. The best churches are places of immense healing.

During this time, a fundamental truth struck me as my intimate relationship with God grew. I looked at my children and marveled at the extent to which I could love them. I set boundaries for them because I love them. When they break a rule, I don't judge them. I allow them to have consequences so that they learn from their mistakes, but I don't think any less of them for breaking the rule. When I have told my son over and over and he still doesn't listen, I sometimes allow him to do things that I know may end with him falling down and suffering a few scrapes and bruises. I figure he's not going to learn any other way because he's not listening to me. So I just stay close enough to keep him from getting hurt too badly and allow him to experience some bumps in the road.

As I grew with God, I began to see a relationship with Him along the same terms. I am a child of God. If I, as a human, have the capacity to love my children as much as I love them, what kind of capacity must God have to love us? There is absolutely nothing my children can do to make me not love them and want the best for them. God feels the same way about each of us but on a supernatural level. Really understanding and internalizing this concept, this picture of an amazing love of God, truly changed my life. It filled that space I had cleaned out in this time of transition with the most amazing light. The darkness that I once carried with me was now transformed into the complete opposite. I sought spiritual advice from all sources- the pastor, books, prayer, meditation, and so on. While I had been in church for most of my childhood and sporadically during my adult life, for the first time ever I understood the love of God. I am humbled by the experiences He has given me. I ask His help every day. I take my mistakes to Him and ask His forgiveness and guidance to choose better next time. I strive every day to live in His love and, in so doing, live a beautiful life.

I didn't realize when I set out on the journey that cleaning out the darkness of my life would lead me to God. When I walked around with so much hurt and darkness, the idea of a relationship with God made me extremely uncomfortable, even anxious. Steve Jobs once said that you can't connect the dots looking forward; you can only connect them looking back on your life. Looking back, I can see how God's plan for my life has always been exactly right, even when in the midst of it, I thought it was all wrong. It was perfectly imperfect. I encourage you, as you go through the process, to seek the spiritual counseling that works for you. If you find yourself in a place of sadness and darkness, don't expect it to change overnight. Just work with your Board of Directors, including your spiritual advisor, to chip away every day at the darkness. I promise you that God is reaching out to you, and He will never lose patience in trying. In His perfect timing, we all come around.

Today, I attend church regularly because I get through my week better if I can get a dose of the presence of God. At this point in my life, church is a very healing place. God often speaks to me in church. But God is not confined to church. He is in nature. He is at work. He is in our bedrooms. He will find us wherever we are. I see now that God started working on me a long time ago. I also found that God had placed people and things in my life all along the way so that I would have the message I needed at exactly the time I needed it to help shed light on my self-deception or help me take another step along the staircase. I learned to follow my instincts. If I had an instinct, a nagging feeling that I should pick up a book, I would do just that. If a certain person kept coming to my mind, I would eventually reach out to that person.

I find that God gives us all the tools. They are all there and He will lead us to exactly where we need to be at exactly the right time. To this day, I meander between churches or yoga classes or even therapists and coaches. I don't think too much. I just go to the place that feels right at the time. I find when I do this, God shows up in big and powerful ways. I believe for you, God has done exactly the same thing. I am confident if you look around at the people, places and things in your life, you will find exactly what you need to take that next step.

I encourage you to surrender to your feelings and instincts and don't think too much about it. If you're led to pick up a reading, do it! If a certain class is on your mind, take it! If an old friend is on your mind, call him! I had to learn to be still and patient enough to listen. God has used many people in my life to give me His message. Many, I believe, didn't even know what a profound impact they had on me, not the least of whom are my children. God speaks to me often through my children. I think this is because they will just say or do what He says because they don't have the ego built up to talk themselves out of the will of God. In many ways, our children are much smarter than we are. They live from a place of immense love and are often, literally, little puppets for God. Be open to the light that is being shed upon your path, no matter the source. The Universe will use your openness to help you find exactly the right way for you.

MOVING FORWARD

The Separation

SOMETIMES people come to me asking for a "legal separation". There is really no such thing in Florida. Many states have abolished legal separation. It is basically a court order resolving child custody and support, visitation schedules and alimony. The court order doesn't actually divorce the couple, and they remain legally married. The sentiment behind the request for a legal separation is a good one. Generally, I think what people are really saying is that they want some space, they want physical and emotional distance from the other party, but they aren't ready to actually get divorced. They aren't sure they want to dissolve the marriage. This is a very logical way of thinking. It was a good idea to separate as I was working through my issues with my Board of Directors.

If you have been living in a dysfunctional marriage, you need to give some serious thought to separating. This means just that. It is clear to me that a couple that "separates" in the same house, generally encounters a significant amount of drama. I find that often things have been done or said in the powder keg of common living quarters that make not only the divorce process infinitely more difficult, but also make it more difficult to co-parent moving forward. The fact is that you have been fighting with your spouse for a long time. If you hadn't, then you probably wouldn't even be contemplating a divorce. At this point, "fighting" has become a habit, the most natural way the two of you interact. Therefore, it is my opinion the process is much more likely to succeed if the parties can truly separate. This means they physically separate, they emotionally separate and they interact only as is absolutely necessary for the children.

There will be time to attempt to come back together. But the two halves need to get healthy so that, if you try to come back together, it is two healthier halves making a healthier whole. In my experience it is really hard to turn the focus inward and do the necessary work of the initial stages when you are living in the same house and constantly interacting with your spouse. It is also my experience that when people move immediately into divorce without a separation period they extend this conflict into the legal system. They tend to have no control over their emotions and their divorce becomes messy and expensive because they cannot separate legal from emotional issues.

During the separation process, my Husband and I most definitely had some growing pains. We were not at a place where we could sit down and talk about anything. We had vastly different views of our marriage and when we tried to talk it just ended up in a huge fight. Eventually, I asked him to give me some space and room to breathe. I couldn't deal with the nature of our relationship at the time. He was a fireball of energy and emotion, and it was really easy to get caught up in that maelstrom. I needed some time and distance to disengage and rebuild. I couldn't deal with the pain and maintain a clear head to have a productive conversation with him. So, I created very clear boundaries in our relationship. Anytime he crossed those boundaries I stopped the conversation and walked away.

I then began changing my external environment. I bought new locks and made it very clear to my Husband that he was not to enter the property. I also changed the furniture and bought a new bed. I surrounded myself with things that were soft and comforting, things that I liked. I made a space for me that was without compromise. It wasn't what "we" liked. It was what I liked and what made me feel at home. It may seem trivial, but it helped to create a good space in which to live.

Now, from the outside looking in, my Husband did not understand. He took it personally. He thought I was "moving on", getting rid of any remnants of our life together. He was resentful, hurt and, finally, angry. He accused me of being financially irresponsible and questioned my choices and, thereby, my ability to care for the boys. After all, he said, "I can't take care of them if you fall apart." My first thought was that I truly didn't remember his cajones being that big. The angry, unproductive part of me said, "He never worked, was a financial drain on the family, spent money meant for formula on beer and cigarettes, blah, blah. Who was he to question how I spent money I'd earned?" Rather than express these thoughts that were just as angry as the statement that spawned them, I pushed those thoughts to the side and tried to look at it from his perspective, with only the facts he had before him. I understood how he could have that point of view. So, I took a deep breath and worked to not take it personally when he expressed his feelings. I listened, nodded in understanding, and kept going.

On some level, he wanted to fight with me. He wanted me to have that reaction out of anger. He was having feelings of abandonment and hurt and didn't know how to process them except to try to pick a fight with me about it. I worked very hard to see this for what it was and to respond appropriately. Often the best thing to do was to just keep my mouth shut. I wasn't always strong enough to say the right thing. As I filtered my thoughts, I found that most of them were angry, snarky responses. As a result I discovered that nodding and saying, "I understand your feelings" was usually a good solution. I probably owed him an explanation, but I couldn't give it to him. I wasn't ready to share with anyone the memories I was having and certainly didn't trust him enough to share.

I don't want to give the impression that I always did the right thing. I certainly did not. In the moment I found out my Husband was cheating, I indulged myself in a bit of fury. In his defense, he would say that he wasn't "cheating," he was having a sexual conversation with a woman on the Internet. In my mind, the two were the same thing. I came home from taking our son to school and the conversation was left open on the computer. By the time he returned home, I'd memorized the entire exchange and repeated it back to him word for word without looking at the computer. I packed his things, put them in the street, gave him $100 and told him he could go live with her. This was not my proudest moment.

His perception is that I abandoned him, that I would let him move away and never see his kids. He turned himself into the victim because he had some tough times after we separated. I paid for a hotel room for him for a few months. I gave him the car that was paid off, continued to pay his cell phone and his car insurance, etc. But, I didn't make him comfortable. I was in a precarious situation because I couldn't enable him any longer. He needed to know that I wasn't going to be there to pick up the pieces. He could not wallow in his disease any longer but he had to pick himself up and fend for himself. He will tell you that he was a stay at home dad who was left to starve, homeless on the street because I was angry that he cheated and refused to support him.

I am not sure which of these perceptions is more accurate. Perhaps I was making the decision not to continue to support him out of anger and spite. I don't believe this to be true. I was in crisis mode and I needed to take care of myself and the boys first. After all, if I fell apart financially, he would not be able to take care of the boys. We had only been married for six years which, in Florida, isn't a long term marriage warranting traditional alimony. And I did help him, just not to the extent he would've liked. He was angry about my decision for a very long time. Perhaps he is still angry. He never showed his anger to the boys. I commend him for always lifting me up for the boys and telling them what a wonderful Mother they had. I told them the same thing about their Father.

During these initial phases, I occasionally received texts from my Husband, usually into the evening and, I can only guess, after he'd been drinking. At this point, I don't remember the actual content of most of them. But, they were angry. It was basically his attempt to convince me of his perspective on the marriage and how I had done things wrong. If I responded by sharing with him my perspective, then I found it always led to a fight. I knew how to push his buttons and he knew how to push my buttons. If I didn't respond or react, he would go right for the jugular and tell me how I had failed as a Mother. This was always very hard to hear. And, when someone says something hurtful to you like that, you want to lash out in return. Sometimes I did, but it never made me feel better. It just made a bigger, angrier mess of things. It just made him come back with more, and it was a never ending slugfest to see who could hurt the other the most until one of us got the last word. I quickly realized that if I kept that up I was going to hate him and that hatred was going to affect our boys. So, as hard as it was, I just stopped. On those nights that he began with the texts, I would read the first one and delete it. Then, every other text that came in that night I would delete without reading it. There was no point in getting caught up in that. It was, very simply, a distraction from my healing.

The intention to disengage

It takes two people to fight. Your spouse does not have to be mature for YOU to move forward with the healing process. Separation, at this point, has nothing to do with your spouse. This is about you. How are you going to change YOUR thinking through this process? How are you going to find happiness for YOU? You don't need your spouse's cooperation to move forward productively, and the fact is, she may never cooperate. That is okay. She may want to wallow in misery for the next two decades. Is that any reason at all for you to do the same?

When you choose happiness, your spouse, who has probably never seen you happy, will not know how to deal with you. The two of you will have to invent a different way to problem solve because he will be dealing with a different person. He will try to push the old buttons. He will try to get you to fight with him again. If you have done your work, you will see this for what it is … the old way of dealing with one another. It is a sign that he still needs to do some work. It is no longer what you choose for yourself. You have chosen happiness, and when you are happy, you hear things differently. The things your spouse says no longer inspire the same reaction. You don't take those words so personally. And you don't react. You understand it has everything to do with your spouse and nothing to do with you. Your spouse may continue these efforts for a time and you will continue to allow him that. After all, it is his path and you can be patient because you love your kids enough to give him all the time he needs to get it right.

During this time, I lived with the intention to disengage from the fight with my Husband. I worked to recognize when he was trying to start a fight with me. I strived to resist the urge to fight with him because I was angry or hurt or because I wanted to be reminded of the reasons we were separating in the first place.

Most of the time we succeeded in avoiding a big fight, but it was really hard. I often found myself saying to my Board of Directors the things I wanted to say to him. This proved to be much more productive. With time, it became clear to both of us that we were done fighting. And, we'd managed to save ourselves from saying things to one another that were difficult to forgive. We continued to remember that we had a responsibility to parent our children together after this was over, whether we remained married or got divorced. We both learned to function in this new system where our roles and interaction were clearly defined and we were both able to focus on healing instead of fighting.

Visitation During Separation

The most contact my Husband and I had during this period of disengaging revolved around visitation. It was very difficult for us to work out our new roles as parents. I felt a tremendous amount of anger and resentment from my Husband as we disengaged. He was in the middle of a crisis, trying to find a job and a place to live. He was so focused on survival, he wasn't always thinking clearly. I believe on some level he didn't visit the boys regularly because he wanted to make it hard for me. I think he wanted me to fail. He wanted me to see that I couldn't do it on my own so that I would reconcile with him. He wanted to go back to his old life where he stayed home with the boys while I financially supported the family. In his mind, the harder he made it on me, the more likely this was to happen.

Now, my first reaction was to say, "Fine, I don't need your help." (Okay, that is the G-rated version of my first reaction). I was independent and strong and I would prove to him I didn't need him. Here is the problem: maybe I didn't need him, but our boys did. So, I came to him very humbly and asked him to see the boys. I tried not to be accusatory or judgmental when I spoke to him. I swallowed a lot of pride in making these requests. Sometimes it felt like pulling teeth to get him to visit with the boys. It felt as though I was begging him and it is not in my nature to beg for anything. "Why should I have to beg him to help with his own children?" I thought. But when the boys didn't see him, they acted out. They had problems in school. They were sad. I couldn't let that happen. I had to do everything in my power to normalize the relationship between the boys and their Father. Our children needed both of us.

Often he would wait until the last minute to get the boys. This meant I couldn't make plans to be with friends or to date. Was it right? No. But, I didn't say anything to him about it. I forced myself to remain positive, to be excited for the boys that they would get to hang out with their Dad. If I'd shared with my Husband my perception and feelings, he would have become defensive and lashed out. We would certainly have started to fight. And the more reaction and fighting he was able to bait me into, the more he would have done those things. He struggled with the distance between us. If

I'd fought with him, it would have led to more fights. When we miss someone, sometimes we view poor interaction as better than no interaction at all. As a result, fighting with him would have served no positive purpose but would have postponed the healing process.

Therefore, the only option for the boys was to accept his choices and make the best of them. I continued to encourage visitation. I didn't focus on what I thought was "right" but that the boys needed to see their Dad. It was hard. Part of me was vengeful. I was angry because he was intentionally making it hard for me, especially with all the other stuff I had going on. I often vented to my Board of Directors. Eventually, the situation improved. Once their Father became more established and stable, he realized his tactics were not going to work and he stepped up more and more.

It seemed like a long road but the reality is the situation improved much more quickly than if I'd fought with him about it. My intention to disengage, although difficult, worked. I learned something in the process. I learned I'm not superwoman. I cannot be the Mother and the Father no matter how hard I try. Our boys need both of us. It was my job as a Mother to make it a priority to maximize each of our roles as parents.

Victim Mode

In the beginning, my Husband and I each engaged in victim mentality. Often in the initial stages of a separation process, one or both of the parties are stuck in victim mode. Too often people play out their perceived victimization in the legal system. Whether you are moving forward to attempt to save the marriage or moving forward with divorce, your relationship as you know it is ending. Some bad things happened to cause that relationship to end. Maybe absolutely none of these were your fault. There is no excuse for someone cheating on you, hitting you, verbally abusing you, spending money recklessly, etc. However, if you focus your energy and mental capacity thinking about how badly you were wronged, how the other person hurt you, how the other person was unjustified in her actions and so on, you will find yourself on a hamster wheel of unproductive emotions. Understand that, no matter what happened, you had a role in it.

People play out their self-victimization without even realizing it. They carry thoughts like, "I want the Judge to know what he did to me." "It is not *right* that I pay alimony because the divorce is her fault and I was a faithful and obedient Husband." "She doesn't deserve the house because she never paid the mortgage." And so on. Seeking "justice" in Family Law is almost always a by-product of self-victimization. If you deserve "justice" you must be a "wronged" party, i.e. a victim. In the coming chapters, as we discuss the process of divorce, we will talk more about the ways victim mode pollutes the divorce process. However, in the initial stages, victim mode is almost always prevalent. It was for me. I viewed myself initially as the victim of his alcoholism, cheating and addict mentality.

Before we can make a rational decision about the right path moving forward, we have to begin to recognize how we establish ourselves as the victim so we can release that mentality. As long as you are the victim, your power is in another person's hands. It will depend on that person to stop the behavior or the Courts to administer justice in order for you to move on. Too often, people leap into divorce seeking this justice. They are desperate for someone to validate their pain, to tell them, "You were right, he was wrong." I challenge you to change your thought process. The legal system dissolves a marriage using a very un-emotional formula. People are frequently offended by the approach. If you find yourself offended by the lack of emotion in the legal system, you are in victim mode and are not in a place where you can decide which path forward is truly the best for your family.

Princess Diana once said, "We can forgive a lot of things if we are happy." This is the basic tenet of entering a Divorce with Joy. For a decade, people sat across from me, spilled their entire life story and ended with "I'm just not happy in this marriage." Often the true statement is that people are just not happy in themselves. A marriage isn't going to fix your misery or make you happy. If you are happy, a marriage isn't going to change that either. It may be that the marriage isn't functioning, but that isn't a barrier to your basic happiness. So, here the real work begins. Your mission is to find a way to enter conflict in joy. This is, perhaps, the hardest part. Whether you stay married or get divorced, there will be conflict on the horizon. Either you are hashing out the remnants of the old relationship so that you can build a better one or you are hashing out the parameters of your relationship moving forward as a two household family raising children. In either scenario, no decision is properly formed from a place of anger, hatred and hurt.

As you contemplate divorce, you enter a time of transition and transformation. The most successful people don't confine this transformation to the marriage. The people most successful when contemplating a divorce take a full accounting of their OWN (not their spouse's) shortcomings, failures and character defects. They honestly evaluate themselves on their part in the breakdown of the marriage and work to change the things they find within themselves that are not as they wish them to be. Do not accept unhappiness and misery as the only way to get through the process. You cannot choose the behavior of your spouse. You cannot choose how your children or your family will react. You can choose only to walk a path to health and happiness. From a place of happiness, a new way of resolving conflict will emerge. The divorce is no longer the outer manifestation of inner conflict.

Forgiveness

As part of my path to happiness, I had to learn to forgive. My feeling is that, before you can make a logical, rational decision on the next right step, you have to learn to forgive. My road to forgiveness had many components. I started, I suppose, with the concept of learning to forgive myself. I walked around much of my life with a huge amount of shame. I was ashamed of choices I'd made in my personal life. I was ashamed of the person I'd become. I didn't open up to people because I didn't like myself. So I believed other people wouldn't like me either. I was guarded and unemotional. I didn't believe the true me was worthy of love and affection, so I hid behind a façade, a persona.

As I began to unravel the truth of my past, I began to see how the choices I'd made were a natural reaction to the trauma I'd suffered. It wasn't an excuse but an explanation. I began to cut myself some slack as I understood myself more and more. I was often reminded of Maya Angelou's famous saying, "When I knew better, I did better." I worked to let go of shame. I learned to forgive myself for the mistakes of my past. I tell myself I am deserving of love, happiness and good things. I focus on the choices I make today, instead of the ones I made last year or last decade or in my teens. When I make a bad choice, I confess it to a trusted advisor and to God. I ask for forgiveness and guidance to choose better and I move on to today's choices.

Once I developed a kinder internal dialogue, I began the process of forgiving others. The more I remembered about my sexual abuse, the more I began to see how profoundly it has affected my life. I am only beginning to chip away at all the abuse took from me. It has truly shaped my entire existence. The worst thing about sexual abuse is not the abuse itself. The worst thing about sexual abuse is the way your mind has to warp itself in order to preserve sanity and cope with the world. At a very young age, I developed a very tough persona that believed the world was unsafe, that people are ruled by their sexual desires, that people lie, cheat and steal and cannot be trusted. I then created an entire life which reinforced this world view.

As a criminal defense and divorce attorney, I lived a life where I was constantly reminded of the ways in which people can't be trusted or the ways in which they lie, cheat, steal and hurt others. Until very recently, I didn't consciously know I believed these things or how it was affecting my life. I didn't see the persona but believed that it was just "me." I believed that was just how I was. As I look back, the persona was evident in every action and aspect of my life. I lived most of my life without ever being vulnerable to anything or anyone, especially a man. The person that developed over time was not my authentic self. My authentic self is not driven by fear but by love. This person that developed after the abuse, the only version of me I'd ever known, was a protector and a punisher, a person driven almost entirely by fear and anger. This person was guarded, anxious, scared, and unhappy. This guise that developed after my abuse kept me sane (or relatively so) but anytime you live outside of your authentic self, there is dysfunction and drama. I didn't want that for myself any longer.

As I began to see all of this for the first time, I was very angry at my abuser. I was mad that he took away my innocence. I was mad that he took away my Joy. I realized that the only way to get her back, the only way to recapture my Joy, was to forgive him. I could never live my authentic self with hate and anger towards my abuser. I was infuriated because I didn't believe he deserved my forgiveness. In my mind, I could see myself as that little girl and all I wanted to do was throw rocks at him, to hurt him like he hurt me.

I struggled with forgiveness. Not only was I angry with my abuser, I was also angry with God for allowing the abuse to happen. I see now that I didn't trust God all those years of my life, because He allowed this to happen. How could I trust Him? There had been profound pain in my life. I suffered abuse that I had absolutely no part in creating. I was, in the truest sense of the word, innocent. No child ever deserves what happened to me. How could God let that happen? He could've stopped it and He didn't. I was, at least subconsciously, very angry at God.

Often people debate whether humans have free will or are simply acting out God's will. How could God's will be for me to be molested as a baby? I prayed and prayed and searched and searched for a way to soften my heart to forgive God and my abuser. Eventually, I settled on this revelation: We have free will AND we are acting out God's will. I believe both are true. God has a greater understanding than we, as humans, can ever fathom. I don't believe God intended for me to be abused. I believe that act was one of free will of my abuser and he is responsible for that choice and its consequences. However, God took that choice and turned it around to the greatest good possible. Everything in life is defined by its opposite. If we didn't have dark, we wouldn't understand light. If we didn't have bad, we wouldn't understand good. We can only understand true love by experiencing hate or pain. If I'd never lived through pain, how could I ever truly understand how amazing it is to live in love? If I'd never been the subject of my abuser's free will, how would I ever have learned the beauty of forgiveness?

I came to the understanding that, while God would prefer we not make those bad choices, He gave us the will to choose. He could force us to choose well. He could force us to choose Him. But, it is much more beautiful when He doesn't. It is much more beautiful and meaningful when we come to God's will through our own free will. So, God takes the choices of the collective whole and works them for the greater good. He molds each choice so that we eventually arrive at the will of God. And, the other kicker, He loves my abuser as much as He loves me. He loves the murderer on death row as much as He loves the Pope. He may not love the choices of each equally, but He loves their souls equally. After all, I have done things that caused pain to others. Not to the extent of my abuser, but nevertheless, pain is pain. So, if I expect forgiveness for the mistakes of my life, I have to extend that to those who made mistakes against me.

Even knowing these things to be true, I had a hard time truly understanding them and feeling them in my heart. It is one thing to know that you need to forgive, it is quite another to actually find forgiveness in your heart. One day, by chance, I crossed paths with my abuser. He was very excited to see me. I looked in his face and saw love and happiness. My goodness. On some level, he did love me. It was sick and twisted and misguided. What he did to me was an extension of his own dysfunction. I suspect he too was molested as a child, but I don't know for sure. Clearly, however, he learned to express love in that depraved way. But, looking in his face that day, I no longer saw him as a monster, as this evil, greater than life character of my childhood. I saw him as a man, nothing more. He is a man with flaws and pain and struggles, just like the rest of us. Ultimately, he has to live with the consequences of his choices. I do not. I can choose differently. I can choose to let it go. I can choose not to live in the fear and hurt and anger that were created by his actions. I can choose to capture again the Me that came here the essence of love and joy and grace. I can choose forgiveness. It is not for him. It is for me.

And, so, I make that choice. I make that choice every day. It doesn't happen in an instant, but it does happen if you commit to the choice. Now you may ask what this has to do with my separation from my spouse. Well, forgiveness is the same no matter the act that you are forgiving. In your marriage, there are things that must be forgiven. Maybe they were your actions, maybe they were your spouse's actions, maybe both. You must, at once, forgive yourself and forgive your spouse. Whatever your path to forgiveness, you have to walk it.

Once I forgave myself, God and my abuser, it was pretty easy to forgive my Husband. He made some choices that hurt me, but I see now that my relationship with him was just a natural consequence of the personality I developed as a result of my childhood trauma. I participated in that marriage and all its hurts and transgressions equally. I chose to marry a man in active addiction so that I could focus on his problems and not deal with my own. I chose to marry a man who had difficulties with intimacy so that I didn't have to deal with my own intimacy issues. Throughout my entire marriage and much of the separation process, I thought it was him. For a long time,

I thought it was my Husband's fault the marriage ended. After all, he is the one who cheated, he is the one who ————————. (It really doesn't matter how any of us fill in this blank. Blame has no place in the equation. As long as we are filling in that blank with anything, we don't get it.)

Then one day I realized, he was no more or less broken than I. We were both a mess. After all, if you find yourself married to a mess, it, by necessity, means you are a mess too. If you weren't, the two of you wouldn't have been attracted to one another in the first place. No emotionally healthy person is going to be attracted to a train wreck. At the end of a very long and arduous process, I came to a sober realization. All the problems of our marriage were just as much my fault as his. And so, I let it go.

Today, I love my ex-husband very much. I probably love him more now than I did when we were married because I now, truly, have a capacity to love. (Although to be perfectly candid, I get on his nerves and he gets on mine. It is, I suppose, more of a sibling-like relationship.) I love myself, for the first time in my life, and therefore I now authentically have the capacity to love him. It wasn't until I arrived at this place that I was able to make a decision as to whether or not I should stay married. For me, the answer was no. We simply were not compatible.

It is an undeniable truth that I was not the same person one year after our separation as I was when I chose him as a Husband. As I continued therapy, I inched closer and closer to my authentic self. However, this put me further and further from the person who was married to this man. We discussed marriage counseling, but it never happened. I don't believe any amount of counseling would've saved the marriage. As I grew in understanding of me, I knew he was not the Husband for me. It isn't his fault or my fault, it just is. And, therefore, we moved forward with divorce.

About a year after we separated, I drafted the divorce papers. I mailed them to him. We discussed it and came to an agreement on all of the issues. We had genuine disagreements on how things should look going forward, but we each expressed our positions and arrived at a middle ground. He was very mature about the legal divorce process. I have no insight on how difficult it was for him, but I assume it was excruciating. We each dealt with the end of our marriage independently. I didn't try to convince him of my truth and he didn't try to convince me of his. It was very sad, but beautiful at the same time. I am proud of the way we handled the last days of our marriage. Our divorce process took, from filing to final judgment, 34 days.

Divorce?
Can I wait until I am firmly established in the healing process to file for divorce?

Only an attorney in your jurisdiction can tell you for sure whether there is an emergency situation which requires you to immediately file for divorce. If, after careful evaluation of your own motives and feelings, you have a doubt as to whether or not you should file, then you should without hesitation speak to an attorney in your area about your case. These are some common examples of instances in which you may not have the luxury to wait because there are legal or safety interests that can only be protected by filing a divorce.

1. **DOMESTIC VIOLENCE**. If at any point you or your children are seriously threatened, you must move forward with either filing a divorce or seeking an injunction for the protection and safety of your family. I have written in other portions of this book about proceeding with caution when making accusations of abuse. There are times people use the allegation of violence as a mechanism for gaining the upper hand in a divorce to the detriment of the children.

However, the break-up of a marriage is a very dangerous time for those who have been in an abusive relationship. In such an instance, a person shouldn't hesitate to get all the protection the law can afford. Only once there is a measure of safety can a person move forward with the therapeutic process and continue the process of Divorcing with Joy.

2. **ABSCONDING WITH CHILDREN.** If your spouse has threatened to leave the state with the children or has actually absconded with the children, you must act swiftly. Most states have a radius restricting the number of miles a parent can move with the children without following a clearly defined legal process. When the children are removed from the jurisdiction, it is vitally important to move quickly to protect your legal interests and your parental rights. In this instance, you should seek advice quickly from a trusted legal advisor and decide on a course of action specific to your situation.

3. **DISSIPATION OF ASSETS.** If you find yourself in a situation where a significant amount of money or other asset has recently disappeared, then you may need to move forward with a divorce to freeze the remaining assets and/or order the spouse to return the asset which has disappeared. The more time that passes, generally, the harder it is to recover an asset. After all, the Judge can't order the party to return money that was long ago spent or an asset that was long ago sold. Along the same lines, if you have been a parent working in the home for so many years that you no longer have any marketable skills in the workplace and need financial assistance from your spouse, then you may need to immediately file for divorce to request Court ordered support payments. Court orders don't normally happen overnight and parties sometimes can't financially afford to delay filing the divorce while they move through the initial phases of the separation.

As an aside, I encourage people not to get themselves in this situation. Whether you are working for pay or not, you should always be responsible with money and for yourself. You should always have your own money and savings. If your spouse is so controlling that you're not allowed to have your own nest egg, then become resourceful. I've seen people who got cash back every time they went to the store and built a nest egg in that way. Or, those who bought items which their spouses approved and then returned them for cash. You cannot legally hide funds once the divorce process begins, but there is nothing to say that you can't build yourself a layer of protection during the marriage in case an emergency ever arises. In any event, sometimes finances play a significant role in deciding whether or not to proceed in a divorce. This is also one of the areas that a mal-intentioned divorce attorney can most easily exploit. Your Board of Directors will be most valuable in helping you evaluate the true necessity/emergency and act accordingly.

These are common examples of scenarios that may require a person to file for divorce when he would otherwise have the luxury to wait. It is certainly not an exhaustive list. There are as many different divorce situations as there are people. However, when you are trying to get an honest evaluation as to whether you can wait or must move forward with divorce for a legal reason, it is vitally important to be mindful of the types of attorneys. Use the tools outlined in the latter chapters to choose an attorney who will give you an honest evaluation of your case and of the true risk involved if you decide to delay the divorce.

Drama vs. Abuse

All abuse situations have drama, but not all drama situations are abuse. There is, in the context of a separation and potential divorce, your regular run-of-the-mill drama. This is general arguing and moving through conflict out of emotions like hurt, anger and fear. It is normal and not rooted in deeper psychological issues. Then, as a completely separate beast, there is the abusive relationship. Now, whether or not you identify yourself as a person who has been abused, I encourage you to read this chapter. I lived almost my entire life not identifying myself as an abuse survivor. For the vast majority of my life, I didn't have any conscious memories of my sexual abuse. But, the situation goes deeper. Until very recently, I have always lived in an abusive relationship of one kind or another. The problem is, when you know nothing but abuse, it is hard to see it for what it is. It is just the way things have always been.

My parents divorced when I was five. I then lived primarily with my Mother and had visitation with my Father every other weekend, a couple of weeks during the summer, split Holidays, etc. My Mother is bipolar and also exhibits obsessive, compulsive qualities. She is currently medicated and has functioned very well for the last 10-15 years. However, she went undiagnosed, and therefore without medication, until I was 20 years old.

As a result, during my childhood her disease caused her to behave in ways that were very detrimental and hurtful. She kept a disturbingly immaculate house. People would come to our home and exclaim that it looked like no one lived there. It was that perfect. This is with a 7 year-old and a 5 year-old living there. Having children who are that age now, I realize what it took to maintain such perfection. We were treated as maids. My Mother was extremely controlling. I have very vivid memories of mopping and cleaning before school. If the bed wasn't perfectly made, my Mother would rip all the sheets off, throw the mattress on the floor and make me do it again. If all the washcloths weren't in the cabinet with the folds facing outward, she would clean the shelf with one swipe of her arm and I would start over with all the towels on the floor. This is all before I ever even made it to school.

I walked around on eggshells not knowing what she would find next that I'd done "wrong." This is the way I lived. I never knew anything different. I didn't know this as mental abuse. I thought that because she didn't beat us to the point of having bruises or neglect us to the point of starvation, that I wasn't abused (at least physically, I see now that we were emotionally starved for love). I mean, she gave us the "best" of everything. She spent an absurd amount of money on us. We always had the latest fashion, the jewelry we wanted, a nice house, etc. There was a lot of pomp and circumstance around the Holidays, with over the top decorations and celebration. Those things were incredibly fun as a child.

As a teenager, when I decided that I wanted to live with my Father, the first thing my Mother said was that if I went with my Father I wasn't going to take anything from her house. It was as if she was bribing me with material possessions. Well, I didn't care about the stuff. I was tired of walking around in all that tension, never knowing what the day was going to be like. The confusing thing for a child is that when my Mother was on the upswing, she was a very fun person. We went on vacations and played and had a "happy" childhood. But, when she was on the downswing, it was bad, and I never knew when the bottom was going to fall out. I was tired of living that way and I didn't care if I went with just the clothes on my back. I had to get out of there. I remember telling myself, "This is no way live." Instinctively, at least I knew that.

I don't want this to be perceived as a bashing of my parents. They did the best they could with where they were at the time. My Mother is much different when her disease is being treated. And, in many ways, my Mother's illness may have saved my life. I had no idea at the time, but I was running from some very deep hurt. The chaos my Mother created was a fabulous distraction from actually remembering, feeling and dealing with the sexual abuse. Therefore, I learned a coping skill that I brought into my adult life. I learned to focus on other people's chaos so that I didn't have to deal with my own. Now, understand, this was all completely subconscious. I see all of this looking back, but I had no idea I was living it at the time.

I also had no idea my Mother was mentally abusive or that her reality was not one shared by the rest of the world. After all, you can't see what you can't see. I continued the chaos pattern into my adult life. I married someone in active addiction, having no idea what that meant. His disease caused him to live in a warped reality and made me think it was normal. His disease tricks his own brain into thinking things are okay that clearly are not. Worse, his disease manipulated me to believing those things right along with him. He didn't do this intentionally or with malice but as an extension of the addict brain. Most of the time, my Husband couldn't see it either. We lived on a roller coaster of chaos created by our complimentary addictions. I didn't know at the time that this was an extension of the same relationship I had with my Mother, but it most certainly was. Both had high highs and low lows. And I now see that both relationships were mentally abusive. I don't fault either person; each was simply living in his/her disease. The beautiful thing is that when I became healthier, it seemed they became healthier too, at least in the way they related to me.

Know that if you'd asked me two years ago if I was involved in any sort of abuse, I would've said, "Absolutely not." I was strong, accomplished, and I could take care of myself. I was mentally resolute and would never allow anyone to take advantage of me or abuse me. As a Family Law and Criminal Defense attorney, I saw victims all the time. I certainly wasn't one of those people. I wasn't that "weak" woman who allowed herself to be hurt. I would've had a very strong reaction if anyone even suggested I was abused in any way. Well, you know that saying, "Thou protesteth too loudly"? If you have a strong reaction to the suggestion there may be abuse in your history and you want to dismiss this entire chapter and move on, then you especially need to do some deep evaluation of your life. What is there that you can't see? There are many, many different levels of abuse and many, many different ways it manifests. Just because you don't acknowledge it, doesn't mean it doesn't exist. So whether you identify with the abuse history or not, I encourage you to have an open mind in evaluating the relationships of your life.

Now, I say again, I am not a psychologist, psychiatrist, or

therapist. So, I cannot diagnose anyone; nor do I have the ability to help anyone heal from abuse of any kind. If you, as the reader, have any idea whatsoever that you may have abuse issues, please seek help from a professional immediately. Reading a book alone cannot deliver you from those patterns. What I share in this chapter is how I have experienced abuse both professionally, as an attorney helping people through the legal system, and personally, as a survivor of sexual and mental abuse.

Physical Abuse

Physical Abuse seems to be the most obvious. When people place their hands on you against your will, it is physical abuse. This is true whether they've done it one time or twenty times and whether they left a bruise or not. In my early career, I worked as a public defender. I often defended cases of domestic violence. In so doing, I noticed a pattern. The people who are the most abused are the least likely to move forward and prosecute their abuser. They are terrified of the person and have often been severely physically injured by their mate. However, they are also the most likely to rekindle or reconcile the relationship. I don't profess to understand that mentality.

My concern with this book is that people who are the victims of serious abuse may take the idea of forgiveness, love and healing to mean that they shouldn't get out of the abusive marriage. Understand that if you have been physically abused, you can and should follow the tenets of this book. You should separate (and I mean truly separate, mentally, physically and emotionally) from your spouse. You should seek a professional, highly trained therapist. You should take advantage of all the protection the law allows for you and your family. Then you can begin to work toward a Divorce with Joy. You deserve your happy ever after just as much as anyone. You may be a long way from it now and it may take longer to get there, but you can live in happiness. When you're living your happy ever after, it will be all the more rewarding. The further you have to go on the journey, the more you appreciate the destination.

Mental Abuse

From what I have observed, physical abuse generally has a mental component. The mental abuse is the "honeymoon" phase where the abuser sells the story that everything is going to be great and he will never do it again. The abuser also makes the abused believe it is her fault or that no one else will ever want to be with her. For me, the mental abuse wasn't so blatant. It wasn't insults or screaming or anything that fit my traditional view of mental abuse. My Husband's disease deceived him. Therefore, he was constantly deceiving me. He was so wrapped up in self-deceit that it was easy to believe his version of reality. His disease has a bad habit of rewriting history. He remembered things differently than I remembered them and was so convinced of his reality that I believed I was crazy. It is the kind of thing that makes you question everything you know to be true. His disease hides from his conscious brain how bad things are and rewrites the world in a way that makes sense to him to continue in active addiction.

I see now it wasn't all that different from my Mother's disease, and the way it manifested was very much the same. It was a chaotic roller coaster living with great days and terrible days with no advanced warning as to which is coming along next. I became very accustomed to living in fear, fear of what I would find when I got home, fear that this day would be a bad one, that the bottom would fall out any minute. This is, I believe, on the mild scale of mental abuse. Many, many people deal with mental abuse on the other end of the spectrum, where they have no self-esteem left and feel they can't think for themselves. No matter where you find yourself on the spectrum, don't discount it. Mental abuse of any severity has to be addressed before a person can move forward productively.

Resources

I must admit, I am woefully unqualified to address abuse issues. I can only tell what I experienced and have witnessed. But, there are many people out there well qualified to help you identify if you are an abuse victim and how to move forward. If there is any question in your mind, I encourage you to do some research in your area to find people who can help. Nationally, there is the National Domestic Violence Hotline which is open 24 hours a day, 1-800-799-SAFE, the National Resource Center on Domestic Violence www.nrcdv. org, Futures without Violence and The National Coalition Against Domestic Violence. For sexual abuse survivors, there is the National Sexual Assault Hotline 1-800-656-HOPE run by RAINN (Rape, Abuse and Incest National Network). These organizations can direct you to help in your area. Either way, it is important to distinguish abuse from drama because the nature and extent of the help needed throughout the process will vary based on where you find yourself on the spectrum.

It was necessary for me to have a certain level of professional help. There is no shame in needing help with your healing process. What has happened to us is not our fault. How we participated in it is worthy of forgiveness. We didn't know what we were doing at the time. The only thing that is our fault is what we do once we have seen. I made many choices in life that do not paint me in the best light. I know now that I was acting in the way that many abused people behave. I cannot beat myself up for that or for needing help to behave differently in the future. I am responsible for my choices moving forward, however. Now that I see how my past has impacted my life, if I refuse help and continue to move in the same old patterns, I am responsible for the pain I cause, both to myself and my children. My children deserved better and so do I. Your children deserve better and so do you.

Love and Marriage

We reach the point where you've been doing your work. You have completed an honest evaluation of your role in the relationship, and you've evaluated the relationship for abuse vs. drama. You have created distance between yourself and your spouse so you can focus on the process of cleaning out and learning love. You are to be commended because, too often, people who are in the initial stages of separations move forward with hiring an attorney and starting a full-fledged war with their spouse either out of anger or as a distraction from doing the necessary internal work. I hear people say, "I'll get into therapy after the divorce. I just can't deal with that right now" or, "I'll take some time for myself when this is all over." People commonly file a divorce out of haste and then dismiss it after cooler heads prevail. Unfortunately, I think sometimes marriages that could've been saved are damaged beyond repair because an attorney appeals to the client's anger and starts a legal battle prematurely. Congratulations on choosing a more productive path. It takes great courage to heal. I applaud your effort.

At this point, couples who have each been doing the work outlined in the book can better choose the appropriate route forward for the family. It is a noble endeavor to try to save the marriage. It is neither easy nor the path of least resistance. I encourage each person who has the slightest inkling the marriage can be saved, not to pull the divorce trigger too quickly. Often people are eager to get divorced because they are in pain. They think, incorrectly, that getting divorced will end this pain. It will not. Check your motives and rationale and make sure you are making the decision from a positive place. If you are well established in the therapeutic process and have reached a place of forgiveness, I encourage you to speak to your Board of Directors about the proper next step. If you choose to save the marriage, let it be as healthier individuals who can work towards coming together in a healthier relationship. If ever there was a chance to save your marriage, it is at this point in the process. This is often where people enter into serious marriage or relationship counseling. The marriages that seem to have the best chances are those where the Husband and Wife are at a place to build a relationship which accurately reflects their new-found inner happiness and health.

What if I want to save the marriage but my spouse wants to go forward with divorce?

Under the law, the Judge can't make people stay married if they don't want to be married. Often people come to me and ask if they can stop the other party from getting a divorce, if they can fight the divorce itself (as opposed to fighting about the issues of the divorce). They are basically asking, "Can I go to court and ask the Judge to refuse to grant the divorce at the end of the case?" Conversely, people also ask if their spouse can stop the divorce. They recognize their spouse wants to stay married and are afraid they won't be able to get divorced in the end. Well, the other party can make the process very difficult, but they can't stop the process. If one party believes the marriage is irretrievably broken and insists on moving forward through divorce, then the inevitable result is a divorce.

I see people who don't want to get divorced and decide that, if their spouse is going to get divorced, it isn't going to be easy. They are going to punish them the entire way through the process and make it as difficult as possible. Unfortunately, there are many attorneys who will help them do it. The attorney will create as many obstructions as possible and keep the parties tied up in court for years. The attorney stands to make tens of thousands of dollars "helping" the client "fight" a divorce the client doesn't want. If this is what you are feeling, I encourage you to continue working through the process with the Board of Directors. It is really wasteful to create this mess in the legal system because you are afraid of being divorced. It is not rational to spend such vast amounts of money making difficult the inevitable result. If people are honest with themselves, they find the compulsion to stay married is almost always based on fear. They are afraid of losing their spouse, their spouse's money, their children or their security. They're afraid they'll never be "loved" again and they continue this unhealthy attachment to their spouse. Sometimes it is sheer anger and hurt. Either way, it is not love.

I can't say that I wanted to be divorced. I am confident my Husband did not want to be divorced. Neither changes the fact that the marriage just didn't, nor ever would, work. The entire goal of the first portions of the process and the Board of Directors is to get you to a place of acceptance. Accept your role in the breakdown of the marriage. Accept the proper function of the legal system. Accept your emotions and process them outside of the legal divorce. Accept you are powerless to change anything but yourself and your perspective. Accept that the relationship with your spouse as you knew it is over, and it is time to rebuild a better way of interacting. Accept, accept, accept. If you are truly working from this place, you can also accept your spouse's perspective on the proper path moving forward. You can accept that your spouse wants the divorce (even if you don't) and refrain from wasting money fighting the inevitable result. If you are the person who wants a divorce and your spouse is being difficult or intentionally stalling, acceptance will help you deal effectively with the antics. The more your spouse realizes that she isn't pushing your buttons with the delay, the greater the chance the behavior will stop. Either way, when you arrive at a place of acceptance, you are at peace in the process.

Once you have found acceptance, you can act rationally moving forward in either scenario: A. the process of rebuilding the marriage or B. the process of dissolving the marriage and rebuilding a relationship as unmarried co-parents. If you are moving forward with divorce, it is important to choose an attorney who will act appropriately and help the process be productive. Attorneys can use their expertise and experience to make the divorce therapeutic and

productive. However, there are attorneys who value their own financial gain above the functionality of the family through the divorce.
It is up to you to choose an attorney best suited to work for the best
interests of your family in the legal process of divorce.

THE LEGAL PROCESS
OF DIVORCE

Why did I become an attorney?

GREAT question. You know how you sometimes wake up in life and find yourself in a place having no idea how you got there? Maybe you feel that way as you wake up and find your marriage is a mess. Well, I woke up one day and found myself taking an oath to uphold the Constitution. That is a big responsibility for a girl from South Georgia in her early twenties. Honestly, I had to give some thought to the "why" I became an attorney. Let me first tell you "how" I found myself there.

Some things in life happen without us really having any intention to make them happen. This is how I know that I am Divinely led. Sometimes I imagine God's two fingers on my head leading me through life, pulling me back when I wander off course. I was raised in a small town. By small, I mean no fast food, no traffic signals. By small, I mean kids were driving through town at age twelve because they'd been driving tractors since they were nine. It was small. After seventeen years of small town life, I was ready to go. My ticket out was school, so I blazed through at lightning speed and found myself with a Bachelors degree at twenty years old. In my head I said, "Uh oh, now what?" I didn't have a plan. So, I figured I would continue school. It wasn't as if I could work with a History degree at such a young age. I began to explore my options. Throughout undergraduate school, I really loved diplomatic history and considered pursuing a Doctorate in the field and becoming a college professor. This plan would take another five years. Or, I could go to law school. With a Law degree, I could still teach if I chose, and law school required only three more years of school. Law school won.

To illustrate how haphazard this really was, I remember frantically completing admissions applications on the last day they could be postmarked for submission. My parents didn't go to college and I didn't have anyone to hold me accountable. I was a typical twenty year old. Everything was thrown together at the last minute. A few months later I began to receive acceptance letters. The day I opened the mailbox and received the first "congratulations" letter was so surreal. I thought, "Wow! This is really happening."

I suppose, therefore, the short answer for how I ended up in law school is: Divine Intervention. It truly was a miracle. As I moved through school and into my career, I began to realize why I'd been led there. It is a great honor to speak on another person's behalf. To be a lawyer is to be a storyteller. It is to put yourself in another person's shoes and understand their plight. It is to take that understanding and present it to a judge or jury and make them care. Make them want to help your client. Make them understand your client and want the best for him in the same way you do. To be a lawyer is to stand up for another person, to give them grace despite the choices they've made and to ask others to do the same. It is beautiful and an honor. Lawyers are privileged to be entrusted with their jobs. This is why I became a lawyer.

The next appropriate question is, "Why are you still a lawyer?" In ten years of practice, I admittedly became a little jaded. While I still believe in the reasons I became a lawyer, I don't see things working that way regularly. Attorneys behave poorly. Clients behave poorly. People are ungrateful and entitled. It becomes messy. I became somewhat disenfranchised with the whole system. There were times when I hated my job and wanted to run to the beach to sell coconuts for a living.

However, even in the midst of a mid-practice crisis, I saw

glimpses of beauty in my work. I would have those cases and clients who made me proud to be an attorney. I decided I would grow these experiences. I decided I would only take clients that wanted an attorney who actually helped the situation, clients who wanted to heal. At first, this was very detrimental to my finances. But, I didn't care. All the money in the world was not worth my happiness. I found that the more I focused on this type of client and method of practicing law, the more I loved my job again. My clients were happier at the end of their case. They were better off for the work we'd done. I could look at my kids with a good conscience and know they could be proud of their mom. I began to want to share these experiences with my colleagues, new clients, and the world. Divorce with Joy was born. I am still an attorney because I know we can do better as a profession and as people. I want to do my part to help people find joy in any circumstance. Practicing law allows me that privilege.

How should a divorce attorney practice law?

Divorce can be drama free. Your family can be saved. A divorce attorney's job is to make it happen. A divorce does not necessarily create a broken home. When the parties act appropriately through the divorce process, the end result is not a broken home but two healthy, happy homes and an overabundance of love in which children thrive. The attorneys have an important role in determining how functional the family units will be at the end of the divorce.

There is a reason that people and society in general have distaste for attorneys. I could spend a few pages talking about the ways I believe we, as a profession, have veered off course. But, I think we probably already have a good idea what is wrong with the way some attorneys conduct business. With that in mind, I present my belief on a divorce attorney's role under the law. An attorney takes an oath before beginning the practice of law. Each oath differs to some extent but generally has the following principles. This is a compilation of the oath from a few states:

I will support the Constitution of the United States and the Constitution of this State;
I will maintain the respect due to Courts, opposing parties and judicial officers;
I will employ only such means as are consistent with truth and honor;
I will treat all persons whom I encounter through my practice of law with fairness, courtesy, respect and honesty; I will abstain from all offensive personality and advance no fact prejudicial to the honor or reputation of a party or witness, unless required by the justice of the cause with which I am charged
I will use my knowledge of the law for the betterment of society and the improvement of the legal system;
I will never reject, from any consideration personal to myself, the cause of the defenseless or oppressed, or delay anyone's cause for lucre or malice;
So help me God

Here are some things that may surprise you in the oath of an attorney.

1. We are supposed to be respectful of each other, the Judge, our clients and the other party (i.e. your spouse).
2. We are supposed to tell the truth.
3. We are supposed to use the practice of law for the greater good, the betterment of society and the legal system and
4. We are not supposed to delay a case for our own financial gain.

The oath is not some ideal to which we are supposed to strive, this is how we are mandated to behave from the day we engage in the practice of law until the day we retire. Unfortunately, because clients don't understand how the legal system is designed to work, they demand a certain type of behavior from their attorney. In response to what the client demands, attorneys too often stray from the principles of the oath. However, any time a client insists the attorney stretch the meaning or spirit of the oath, the client will ultimately be dissatisfied with the attorney and the legal system. Understanding the oath an attorney takes before embarking on the practice of law, what, then, should an attorney do in the context of a divorce?

A divorce attorney's job is to fight appropriately based on legal, rational arguments in an effort to serve the best interests of the children. In short, the attorney's job is to fight and the client's job is to heal. The client's obligation is to choose an attorney from a place of love, using the tools of the book. After the client has selected a good attorney, the client should put down his boxing gloves. The client does not have to fight any longer. The attorney can fight the battles and protect the best interests of the family.

The attorney who is practicing appropriately is not emotionally involved in the process and will assist the client in making sound decisions about what is important and warrants further effort. It is the attorney's job to make sure the client's legal interests are protected. When the case arrives at the point where the attorney requires input on how to proceed, the attorney should meet with the client, give him the options, give the pros and cons of each side, give advice on which option the attorney believes is best, and the client will, at that point, make a choice. It is nothing to worry about now. It is nothing to stress over. When the time is right, the client will make the proper decision with appropriate guidance from the attorney. Otherwise, the client's job is to simply heal. Don't fight with the spouse, don't fight with the attorney, don't fight with friends and don't fight the process. Just stop. Make no mistake, if energy is focused on a fight, a parent cannot be connected to the children. Any fight will absolutely disconnect a parent from a child, and the child will suffer for it. This is the bottom line, without exception.

Let me also explain what a divorce attorney's job is not. A divorce attorney's job is not to punish the spouse or act as a battering ram to beat the spouse. A divorce attorney's job is not to "fight" for things the client is unlikely to win or to "fight" to seek justice for the client's emotional grievances. The divorce attorney's job is not to indulge the client's every feeling and perceived transgression. Understand that when a divorce attorney refuses to fight for what the client thinks is "right", it doesn't mean the attorney is weak or is doing the client a disservice. Often these attorneys are the best practitioners because they are willing to stand up to the client and forego their own financial interest to encourage the client to work for the family, even when the client isn't able to see how their perspective is hurting all parties involved.

The divorce attorney's job is to point out legal versus emotional issues. Our job is to work to get the best result possible on the legal issues at the lowest financial and emotional cost to the family and guide the client to other remedies for emotional issues. In its purest form and when the attorney adheres strictly to the promises made in the oath, the practice of law is a beautiful, noble profession. This is especially true through the process of divorce.

Divorce Attorneys

There is something fundamentally flawed about the concept that a divorce attorney makes his or her profit from the size and duration of the fight between two people. It is a tough profession for someone with a conscience to endeavor. I will give you an example. It is December, a notoriously slow month in the divorce business. People who owe money aren't paying because they are buying their kids Christmas presents. No new business is coming in because people are trying to white-knuckle it through the Holidays. The attorney has staff to pay, a mortgage, kids with their own wish lists, etc. So, a potential new client comes in. The client just discovered her spouse had been cheating on her and she kicked him out. However, after a 20-year marriage and with three minor children at home, she is wavering on whether she wants to get a divorce or try counseling. Herein lies the problem.

In many aspects, the divorce attorney is also a sales person. We sell our client's version of events to the Judge, we sell ourselves to the client, and we sell the client on a settlement agreement. We all know that you make the sale while the buyers are there. You let them walk out and there is a 90% chance they are never coming back. It is not that hard to justify giving the hard sales pitch. After all, her Husband did cheat on her. Their marriage will probably never recover anyway. The attorney has a family of his own to feed. The potential client is such an emotional basket case that the attorney can literally steer her in either direction. She doesn't have the emotional fortitude to disagree with whatever suggestion this trusted professional makes to her.

So the attorney has a dilemma. Does he give her the hard pitch, take her $5,000 or $10,000 retainer so that he can pay his bills? Or does he refer her to a trusted therapeutic counselor who can help her through the initial stages of the emotional process so that she can make a sound decision, not out of emotion or fear or anger? If the client leaves, she may never return. She may reconcile or may simply hire another attorney. She may think if the attorney suggests therapeutic counseling, the attorney is "soft" or won't represent her aggressively if she decides to move forward with the divorce. Most often people hire attorneys in the "anger" phase, and these are the thoughts of an angry person. *I need a "pit bull". I need someone who will fight for me. I need a "bitch" of an attorney.* What the client really needs is someone who will fight appropriately, mitigate costs and work in the children's best interest. However, in the anger phase, it is hard for clients to see this fact.

As you can appreciate, there are two very different ways of

handling this client consultation. The appropriate thing is to encourage the client to go to counseling and not to give her the hard sell. How many attorneys will behave appropriately? How many attorneys will forego their bottom line and allow the client to walk out the door without a retainer in hand? There are some, maybe even quite a few. However, the situation illustrates the need for the client to obtain a good measure of self-awareness. Clients need to recognize where they stand in the process and need to have the ability to decipher the kind of attorney with whom they are consulting. Clients also need to recognize when an attorney is feeding into the anger and systematically reject that attorney. They need to understand that, in the anger phase, when the attorney is acting appropriately, the things the attorney says may be uncomfortable to hear. When they are angry, clients should seek an attorney who doesn't tell them what they want to hear but what they need to hear. This person will more likely facilitate a divorce in which the family thrives at the end of the process.

In the course of the practice of law, I have observed certain attorney stereotypes that replay again and again. Recognizing the stereotypes may be helpful for the client in determining which attorney will move the client forward in a productive manner.

ATTORNEY STEREOTYPES

THE Old Attorney — The Old Attorney is one who has been practicing 40 years and hasn't read the law in 20. Some people think age and experience are the ultimate factors to consider when hiring an attorney. It is vitally important to have an attorney with both life and legal experience. The client definitely wants an attorney who is knowledgeable, and the length of time in practice is a good factor to indicate knowledge and ability. However, this is not the only factor to consider.

There are attorneys who are practicing in the past. They know the Judge and they have probably been practicing as long as some of the Judges have been alive. The problem is that the Old Attorney can become complacent over time. There is the risk that these attorneys rely only on experience; without a continued dedication to educating themselves on the changes in the law. Recently, I encountered just such a case with opposing counsel. The attorney filed a document that was legally insufficient. It would have been fine ten years ago, but, according to the requirements of modern day law, it was just plain wrong. Needless to say, he wouldn't accept that he was wrong, and, during a hearing on the subject, argued that it was inconvenient to proceed according to statute (i.e. the law) and suggested I (the attorney who was actually following the law) was just being difficult due to a technicality. Apparently, following the law was now merely a technicality.

In short, this attorney was clearly not serving his client well. He did not appear to be educated or knowledgeable, at least not about modern day law. I daresay he is practicing retired. I can imagine the client hired him because he probably has a good sales pitch. I imagine he can speak at length on the number of cases he has completed and won, and can therefore demonstrate that wealth of experience. However, he practices less competently than many new attorneys. At least new attorneys have an insecurity that gives them perspective on what they don't know. Confidence and ignorance of the law are a dangerous combination for an attorney.

Therefore, it is important to ask an attorney what he or she does to stay current on the law. Don't let the attorney tell you that the bar requires continuing legal education, (*CLE) so the attorney is current on the law. While it is true that CLE is required in most states, if not all, it doesn't necessarily mean the attorney knows the law. Often CLE classes can be taken on any area of the law, not necessarily the attorney's specialty. And, just because someone sits through a class doesn't mean he or she absorbs and learns the subject matter.

It is helpful to question the attorney on technology used in the office. If the attorney is technologically savvy, it is likely that he or she is also abreast of the newest research mechanisms and is attempting to run a state of the art practice. If he or she is still going to the law library to do research, you should probably move along. I work very hard to stay current on the law, and I can promise you the most efficient way is not to sift through stacks and stacks of books. I have not been in a law library since I graduated law school. Everything an attorney needs and more is online. A paperless (or nearly so) practice is a good option.

Other efficient additions to an office are email correspondence and e-fax. It is a client's right to know what to expect and how an attorney runs his or her office. It gives the client an idea of the attorney's ability to problem-solve and how much the case is ultimately going to cost. The more efficiently the office runs, the less the client pays in fees. Another example is dictation. The Old Attorney tends to dictate a letter or motion into a machine and have someone else actually type it out. In such case, the client pays the attorney to dictate, the support staff to actually type, and pays for two or three revisions to get the document right. It is, in my opinion, the essence of inefficiency. The Old Attorney also seems to send correspondence for every single thought. It makes so much more sense for the attorney to spend a minute typing out an email to the client. One hand touches it, and there is no cost for postage or letterhead and no necessity for two or three revisions. This is an example of how efficiency can save time and money. However, for many attorneys, inefficiency is acceptable (if not preferable) because they get paid by the hour not the job.

THE BIG SHOT — Beware of the Big Shot. It has always been a bit of a mystery to me why clients hire these people to represent them. These are the types of attorneys who make me feel dirty. They are almost always men, but there are women attorneys who behave just as poorly. In my mind, however, the Big Shot is a man. It has something to do with the male ego but the Big Shot struts around like an arrogant peacock. He usually wears too much jewelry, has a horrifying comb-over, drives an expensive car and his receptionist is almost always a hot, young blonde. These guys get many, many clients. Not only that, they get many, many clients to pay them lots and lots of money. Yet, in my opinion, they do inferior work. The judges usually don't respect them because they can't just resolve a case without court interference, and they have to make a mess out of every single issue. The money, after all, is in the fight for these attorneys. If they guide a client through a case in a reasonable, rational fashion, they don't make nearly as much money. It is difficult to afford the big office, the fancy car and the gold-digger wives when resolving cases reasonably.

If all of the signs above haven't clued the client in as to the type of attorney he is interviewing, here is the tell-tale sign: If, when a client is consulting with the attorney, the attorney spends much of the time orchestrating plans to mistreat the other party, the attorney will absolutely mistreat the client. Trust me, the attorney has devised just as many plans to swindle his clients and has years of practice implementing those plans.

Over the years, I have watched these attorneys and their clients. It is oddly fascinating to see how the attorney manipulates the client and how the client allows the manipulation to happen. These attorneys are fabulous salespeople, basically over-educated used car salesmen. They sell the client a few ways:

1. *I am rich; therefore, I am the best.* Often people think the most expensive is the best. I don't find this to be true with lawyers. A client definitely doesn't want to hire someone who is cheap. If the attorney is willing to work for less than a reasonable rate, there is a reason. However, there is no justification for a person with a normal divorce (by normal I mean without millions of dollars in assets, marital businesses, or other extraordinary complications) to hire someone who is charging $7,500 or more for an initial non-refundable retainer. Think of it this way, for every dollar spent on a divorce, the children have a dollar less to spend on their college education. Do you really want to hire an attorney who has wasted the future of his client's children? The fact that an attorney has such a lucrative practice is no indication that he is of superior quality with superior skills. Frequently, it is quite the contrary.

2. *I think you should be angry.* Often when a client is meeting with an attorney for the first time, the client is very angry. Anger is a normal and sometimes justified reaction to the situation in which the client finds himself. A mal-intentioned attorney will immediately recognize this anger and use it to her advantage. Typically the client, in his anger, wants someone to share his emotion, to match the anger and fight in court with the same intensity the client wants to fight out of court. The Big Shot will play right into this

desire. The Big Shot will make the client feel good that she is going to pummel the spouse, going to take the spouse to the cleaners. The attorney will sell the promise that the client will be vindicated, will "win" and, in victory, all will be right. The truth is that people lose a lot of money chasing vindication. An attorney should be the voice of reason. An attorney who fights out of anger will always lose. Anger clouds judgment. So, if an attorney loses her cool, she has lost the upper hand in the case. Never, ever does the client want an attorney who is angry and seeking vindication for the client.

The law and the legal system are rational operations. Judges act based on well-reasoned, logical plans presented methodically and without emotion. If the client or attorney is acting based on anger, it will be immediately apparent to the Judge and they will lose credibility. Once credibility is lost, the client will find it hard to get any sort of favorable ruling. Therefore, an attorney who is inflaming or sharing the client's anger is doing the client a disservice. It may seem illogical to the client at first, but the attorney should be unemotional about the client's case. Those who aren't may be more interested in creating a fight and a larger bill than truly serving the client's best interest.

3. *I can give you what you want.* If it sounds too good to be true, it probably is too good to be true. "I have never had a client ordered to pay alimony," says the Big Shot attorney. The clear implication is if you give the attorney this retainer you won't have to pay alimony. I heard a Big Shot attorney discussing a divorce in which alimony was an issue. He stood up in all his glory and gave a five- minute rant about how he had been practicing so many years and never, ever had he litigated a case where the judge awarded alimony. He talked about how he would file this motion and get this testing and blah blah blah. (At some point he

began to sound like Charlie Brown's teacher, and I could no longer understand him.)

However, a light bulb went off for me. Instantly, I understood how this attorney got these clients to pay him so much money. He sold them exactly what they wanted whether he could produce it or not. Clearly, he had given the speech before; I suspect mostly to clients. He understands that people despise paying alimony. So he sells them the dream that they will never have to do it. He is a sure bet. Never has he lost, and if the client just pays him enough, he will make sure there is no alimony. I would bet that the attorney even makes his "strategy" seem attractive financially. I can imagine him saying something like, "You can pay this other attorney $3000 and you are going to end up paying alimony. Let's just presume the alimony you would pay with this other attorney would be $1000 per month. Well, I can't promise you that you won't pay alimony with me, but I can tell you that I have never had the Judge award alimony against my client. So, let's presume you pay me $8,000 but there is no alimony awarded. After five months of you not paying the alimony you would've paid if you hired the cheaper attorney, I have paid for myself and you don't have to write that check for alimony every month for the rest of your life." The client sees it as a win-win. The client doesn't have to do that thing which the client most loathes i.e. write that alimony check.

The issue lies in what the attorney is leaving out. Notice he said, "I have never had the Judge award alimony against my client." While this *may* be true (and I stress *may* because I don't really believe it), the most it really means is that he never took a case to trial where alimony was appropriate. He didn't say no client of his has ever paid alimony. What ultimately happens is something like this. The client pays the attorney an exorbitant retainer. The attorney files multiple motions and appears to be fighting hard against alimony. Then, the retainer is exhausted and the client gives the attorney more money because the attorney is, after all, fighting so hard. Then opposing counsel files an attorney's fees motion and the Judge orders the client to pay his spouse's attorney's fees as well. The client realizes $25,000 is down the drain. The case has become emotionally and financially draining. The attorney then advises the client that the judge is not ruling favorably or new facts have come to light or some other excuse explaining why the client may be required to pay alimony. Then, finally, the client sees that he is going flat broke and will still be paying alimony if he allows this attorney to keep up the "fight". The client eventually settles on a reasonable amount of alimony. The Judge, therefore, did not "award" alimony; the client agreed to it because he finally realized it was an inevitable result. A sensible attorney could have set the client expectations more appropriately in the beginning and the client could have saved his $25,000. The client should have hired the attorney who was going to charge an affordable rate to make a fair evaluation of the case.

4. *I am special.* If ever you find yourself in a consultation and the attorney spends the time telling you how great she is, how no other attorneys can do what she does, or how she is special, be on guard that you may not be with the best attorney for the job. It is generally not considered ethical practice for an attorney to boast about a special relationship with the Judge, but you'll hear things from these attorneys like, "I worked on the Judge's campaign. I play golf with the Judge. I used to work with the Judge." I suppose technically this is a statement of fact and not boasting a special relationship with the Judge. But, the impression is that the attorney can do something that no other attorney can do.

While I understand that in the consultation there is an art to giving the client comfort that the attorney is competent, there is also a line that is too often crossed. The fact is that there is a subset of attorneys who are competent, methodical, and professional. They are not money hungry or flashy. They serve their clients well and work in the client's best interest. You will not hear these attorneys boasting about how they are the best. Family Law is not a complicated legal process. The most difficult part of Family Law, from a practitioner's perspective, is managing the clients. There are many, many attorneys who can handle the legal issues of a divorce well. The client should never pay an attorney more than the average rate because she claims to be the best.

5. *I have nothing good to say about any other attorney.* Never, ever hire an attorney who will speak ill of another attorney. I once received a call from opposing counsel. He indicated that his client previously consulted with another attorney in town. That attorney saw I was the attorney on the case and told the client that I was afraid to go to trial. He told the client he could achieve a great result because, ultimately, I would settle the case at any cost to my client because I was terrified to go to trial. The attorney said if he just pushed it long enough, I would eventually cave. The opposing attorney who phoned found this particularly amusing because he and I had been to trial on cases. He knew my reputation as an attorney did not include any fear of trial. In fact, I dare imagine that over the course of my career I have probably been to trial on more cases than the attorney who was selling such a pitch to the potential client. The attorney would say anything, clearly, to get the client's money.

The lesson is, therefore, that when you feel like you are being given the hard sell, you probably are and with little regard to actual truth. When an attorney speaks negatively about another attorney in the sales pitch to the client, the client should seek other counsel. I can only imagine the things that attorney said to attempt to sign the client up and get an exorbitant retainer. He was, by the way, attempting to charge at least twice the average rate. Reality and truth are no barriers for attorneys like him. While a client may feel some comfort in retaining the "most ruthless" attorney out there, this comfort will be short-lived. If the attorney will lie about another attorney, trash the spouse, or make the hard sell, he will have little regard for the client's best interests over the attorney's own bottom line.

THE ROOKIE – Fill-in-the-blank Family Law forms can be found in most jurisdictions online. Frequently people have the perception that they can fill in the content, file the divorce and everything will work out just fine. Attorneys are no exception. When economic times are difficult, attorneys who generally practice in other areas such as Criminal Law, Personal Injury Law and Business Law decide they need to supplement their income. They will then "branch out" into Family Law because it seems easy enough, there isn't a substantial initial financial investment in software or the like, and after all, the attorney needs the money.

Alternatively, there are attorneys who genuinely wish to practice Family Law exclusively but are new graduates and are in their "trial and error" phase. In either scenario, it is usually a bad idea to hire these attorneys. A new practitioner who genuinely wishes to practice in Family Law should work for another attorney proficient in the field for a few years and learn all the things that only experience can teach. The biggest source of knowledge for a Family Law attorney is not necessarily in the statutes or case law but in practical practice. Experience teaches a Family Law attorney the course a Judge is likely to pursue. Experience teaches how to properly manage expectations for the client. Throughout the course of practicing Family

Law, we learn from the mistakes of others- other attorneys, other clients, other parents, other Judges. This experience helps us serve the clients in an effective manner so that they are ultimately happier with the results. It doesn't make the process easy, but it does make the process less traumatic, serves the needs of the family and allows all parties, children especially, to move forward with less emotional scarring.

As a general rule, an attorney who has worked in the mindset of another practice area is going to have a tough transition into Family Law. Family Law differs from other practice areas in method and mindset. As a general rule, attorneys in many practice areas don't "play nice in the sandbox." They tend to attempt to hide documents, file unnecessary forms and motions, and generally work in a spirit of obstructionism as opposed to cooperation. This may be acceptable in other practice areas where the end result may be a client going to jail, or paying money in the form of a judgment. It may, in those instances, behoove the client to have an attorney who works against the grain and prolongs things as much as possible. After all, the client's end result in those cases may be jail or judgment and the client is in no hurry for either of those things to potentially happen. However, Family Law is different. The process in any type of Family Law proceeding is financially draining and emotionally exhausting. When you have a rookie attorney who is unnecessarily prolonging the process, the damage to the family is increased exponentially. The Family Law process is not, then, a therapeutic process but a traumatic one. The clients become dissatisfied with the system because it didn't work for them. Yet the problem wasn't that the system didn't work for them but that the Rookie attorney didn't work for them in the way an effective Family Law attorney should.

Often the Rookie has an additional problem. The attorney on the Family Law case should be detached from the client's emotions. The attorney should not share the client's anger or hurt and should be able to tell the client "no" and set appropriate boundaries. The client will often attempt to pull the attorney into the client's emotional tailspin. It is easy for the attorney to be drawn in because the attorney wants the client to feel like she cares and wants the client to be happy with the end result. The attorney mistakenly believes this can only happen if she responds to the client's every emotion, feeling or request.

It is sometimes difficult not to become emotionally invested. Each attorney has her own history. We do not operate in a vacuum, and we hear some pretty awful stories. Clients often get divorced because of traumatic circumstances like physical abuse, molestation, disease transmittal, etc. It is tempting to take on the identity as a warrior for the client. The attorney will accept less money than the going rate because she feels sympathy for the client. The Rookie will give the client her cell phone, accept calls on Saturday morning and basically allow the client to run the show. These are all rookie mistakes. Clients who are going through a divorce are generally in such an emotional state that it is difficult to see clearly. They want to talk. They want immediate answers. They want to complain about the spouse's behavior. These are all legitimate needs and part of the healing process. However, the attorney is not the appropriate sounding board for these discussions. This is why we have created a Board of Directors. You have appropriate, healthy outlets for all of those feelings outside of the legal system.

The fact is there are very few things in Family Law that constitute a true emergency. Courts don't work on the weekends. It isn't like Criminal practice where Judges are available around the clock and if you are arrested on Friday you see a Judge on Saturday or Sunday. As a result, the Family Law attorney generally can't do anything for you on weekends. The attorney must maintain time for her own life and that must be sacrosanct. If she does not maintain boundaries and a sense of balance with the client, the attorney cannot remain mentally and emotionally stable enough to continue to practice well.

There is a clause in my contracts requiring the client to enter individual therapy with a mental health professional. If the client talks to the attorney about legal issues and the therapist about emotional issues, the client is inevitably happier with the divorce, has a significantly lower legal bill and a more well-adjusted family post-divorce. The more experienced Family Law attorneys understand the confines of the legal system and that many of the client's grievances are emotional issues. The experienced Family Law attorney will spend time with the client pointing out which of the client's grievances can legitimately be solved in the legal system and which should be referred to the therapist or other member of the Board of Directors. The experienced Family Law attorney will not try to fix the client's life. I say all the time, "I can get you divorced. I cannot make the world right". The truth of the matter is the state of the client's world is directly related to the client's perspective as opposed to the actions of the spouse, Judge or attorney. The Rookie will entertain the emotional expressions of the client, address them and attempt to have the Court address them.

By contrast, the experienced attorney is not uncaring but understands that neither the attorney, nor the legal system in general, has a solution for the emotional issues. The experienced attorney gently directs the client to a person who is trained in dealing with the emotional aspect of the divorce and can truly serve the client well in that area. The experienced attorney maintains appropriate boundaries with the client. The client may be resistant initially, but over time, the client takes solace in the fact that the attorney is calm, in control and unemotional. The client will look back on the case and realize the attorney did the client a service by saying no to requests born out of emotion and will be happier with the end result. The client may not like the attorney throughout the entire process, but in the end, the client is hiring an advisor not a friend.

If the client is too close to the attorney, she doesn't have the best representation. It may seem counter-intuitive, but it is absolutely true. The client should not seek out an attorney who always says "yes" but someone who gives an honest evaluation. The client needs an attorney who gives the client both sides of the argument and suggests a course of action that may not be what the client wants to hear. In this scenario, the client knows he has an experienced Family Law attorney.

FLAT FEE DIVORCES – Many people believe a flat fee divorce is the way to go and the attorneys who advertise on television are the best. It must be tempting, from a client's perspective, to choose an attorney who works for a flat fee. Flat fee divorces have some selling points. First, the client's costs are predetermined so it probably gives the client some comfort that the attorney can't gouge him with every invoice. It can seem like a financially responsible decision. However, I have a different perspective. First of all, it is good for the client to have some parameters on the attorney's time. I have found, with a flat fee divorce, clients have no boundary. They call the attorney endlessly with every emotional issue of the day. It is very hard, when there is no monetary value attached to the attorney's time, to separate the emotional aspect of a divorce and the legal aspect. No matter how good or kind the attorney is, the attorney may be your counselor at law but the attorney is not your therapist. Additionally, the attorney is not going to be around forever. The client must learn to work through emotional issues. The client should not be dependent on the attorney to get through the day or even to get through life. It is tempting because attorneys can be empathetic and strong. Often after you speak to your attorney, you feel better. But, this doesn't change any of the facts listed above. In order to facilitate using the attorney appropriately, it is good for the client to be billed for every phone call and letter and work done on the case. It forces the client to evaluate whether the issue is really important long term and whether it is one appropriate for the legal system.

A flat fee divorce should only ever be considered on a case in which the parties enter the legal proceeding agreeing on the terms of the divorce and the attorneys are hired to draft the paperwork in a way that reflects the parties' agreement and protects each party's interests. In these cases, the attorney is simply formalizing a contract between the parties (the Marital Settlement Agreement) and the case doesn't proceed with mediation or hearings.

There is a second issue with flat fee divorces. Often attorneys advertise these at very inexpensive rates. The fact is, in so doing, the attorney is banking (quite literally) on bringing in volume to compensate for the fact that they are doing the divorces inexpensively. This often means the cases are not getting the individual attention they deserve. The divorces take longer than they should. Keep in mind, the longer the divorce, the longer the emotional strife and the greater the emotional fallout for the parties. You can bet this attorney will not return phone calls and will not be quick to react if any unusual issues arise. Firms who routinely engage in flat fee divorces may very well be "mills" that are about volume not quality.

The other alternative in a flat fee divorce attorney is to overcharge each client because the attorney understands that some will ultimately require much more work than the amount charged and some will come in under the amount of work charged. If everybody pays more then, in theory, it will even out over time. So in my opinion, it is a better choice to simply pick an attorney who will handle the case for a traditional fee contract in a professional and appropriate manner. With the tips in this book, the client should be able to find just such an attorney.

How do I evaluate an attorney?

What if you're meeting with an attorney and the attorney doesn't seem to fit any of these personality types, how can you know that he is a good attorney for you? I want to give you some guidance regarding productive questions to ask a prospective attorney and how initial consultations work.

Here is a list of questions with model answers that should help you better evaluate your attorney.

1. *What do you see as the issues in the case? What are the arguments against me on each issue? Is there law to support the counter argument? How have you seen the Judge rule on the issue?*

   The attorney should be able to give you an outline of the issues that will be decided. The outline should be simple, straight forward and easy to understand. Then the attorney should be able to explain the argument of each side in the case. The attorney should also be able to tell you the law and how the law applies to each person's argument. Lastly, the attorney should be able to tell you how some Judges have ruled on this issue. Keep in mind, in most jurisdictions, if the divorce hasn't been filed, the attorney won't know which Judge will be assigned to the case. However, you should be able to get an idea of the strengths and weaknesses of your case based on this conversation.

2. *Will you give me your cell phone number in case of emergency?*
   No matter how badly you would like to have unfettered access to your attorney, the answer to this question should be "no". There should be a mechanism by which the attorney can be reached in case of emergency but the client should not have the attorney's cell phone. For example, in my office, when a client calls and leaves a message, the message is automatically transcribed and emailed to the entire staff within minutes. Therefore, if the client calls at night or on the weekend with what the client perceives as an emergency, I can confirm the evaluation and call the client back if it is a true emergency or wait until normal business hours if the client is acting emotionally. However, an attorney who puts himself "on call" for the client 24 hours a day, 7 days a week is doing the client a disservice. It either shows a lack of understanding for how the process works most effectively or that the attorney plans to

unnecessarily inflate the bill with emotional phone calls. Either way, I would suggest not hiring an attorney who shares his cell phone number.

3. *How do you feel about mental health counseling?*
   Every Family Law attorney should encourage clients to enter individual therapy. A therapist is about half the price per hour of an attorney and is much better suited to handle the emotional aspects of a divorce. If a client is in counseling, it becomes much easier for the attorney to work with the client in identifying the legal aspects of a divorce versus the emotional aspects of a divorce. If a client begins a list of emotional grievances, I am able to gently interrupt and point out that while their feelings are absolutely valid, this issue is one better discussed with the counselor. This saves the client from venting to me at $300+ per hour when I have no ability to solve emotional problems. It is a very effective tool to manage cost, and clients are ultimately happier when they have a better idea of the way the legal process works. If an attorney wants to solve problems, as opposed to creating fights, the attorney will encourage the client to engage in therapeutic counseling.

4. *How much will the case ultimately cost?*
   Now we have reached the million dollar question. You should always ask the attorney this question but understand you are not going to get the answer you want. No attorney should cap cost. The attorney, truly, has no idea how much the case will cost. If you call the attorney every day and speak to her for thirty minutes about every possible contingency and every perceived wrong committed by the other party, your case will be monumentally expensive. The attorney should explain this in the initial consultation. Additionally, no attorney going

into a divorce can know for sure how a case will ultimately resolve. The attorney should tell you that if you are able to negotiate and reach a full agreement before trial, without a hearing, your case will be significantly less expensive than if you fight things out in court. The attorney, in answering this question, should present ideas and suggestions on ways to keep the costs down. If, on the other hand, you get an answer like "As much as it takes to get you what you want," or "Every divorce costs at least $10,000," you should seek other counsel. The entire process should be geared towards giving the client every incentive to use logic over emotion to amicably resolve the issues between the parties.

5. *Do you have children?*
   Understanding this may be a controversial stance, I believe the best attorneys for a divorce are those who have kids of their own. Whether or not the attorney has children should not be the decisive factor in your choice of attorney, but I do think it should be a factor. You cannot explain or rationalize or understand what it means to have children. It is something you must experience to comprehend. I think Fathers and Mothers often make better divorce attorneys. An attorney with children can relate to the clients much more effectively. This is not only due to the higher level of understanding, but also because parents better understand and can foresee logistical problems. An attorney with children has placed children in school, taken them to the doctor, coordinated extra-curricular activities, etc. Those attorneys tend to be more effective advocates for the best interest of the children through a divorce.

6. *Do I have to be tied up in court forever?*
   The answer to this question should be no. The attorney should give you solutions for resolving your case without

going through a long, drawn out process. One such solution commonly used is mediation. In many jurisdictions, mediation is required prior to attending a hearing before the Judge. At mediation, the clients, their attorneys (if they have one), and a neutral third party sit down to attempt to reach an agreement on the issues of the case. Mediation works, but you need to make sure that your attorney is one who believes in the process and facilitates amicable resolution instead of perpetrating disagreement.

I once heard the following story from a very experienced mediator for whom I have enormous respect. He says that too often he realizes that his evaluation of the facts of the case is the first time some clients have ever heard an impartial analysis. He spoke of one Husband who had been married for over twenty years and earned an income four times greater than his Wife. At mediation, the mediator discussed his evaluation that this was clearly an alimony case. (By the law at the time, any attorney, no matter how inexperienced, would recognize that the Husband would probably be paying alimony.) Clearly, the Husband had never heard this news before mediation. His very experienced attorney apparently never clued him in on the fact that the greatest likelihood is that he would be paying alimony. The attorney recognized the client didn't want to hear that he would have to pay alimony so the attorney told the client what he wanted to hear as opposed to what he needed to hear. The attorney said whatever she had to say to get the client signed up and get the retainer in the bank.

The mediation, then, becomes nearly impossible because the Husband had not been educated with realistic expectations from the beginning. The divorce was prolonged, therefore costing more money. The only people who win in those situations are the attorneys. Accordingly, make sure you have an attorney who is encouraging mediation or some other form of dispute resolution short of court. Talk to the attorney about mediation. The attorney should tell you that the vast majority of cases resolve at mediation. The attorney should say that it benefits you to solve your problems instead of placing those problems in the hands of a Judge who doesn't know you, your situation, or your children and who will be working on only the admissible evidence that can be received in a short amount of time. Granted, the attorneys receive much less money on cases that resolve without trial. So, discussing the issue of mediation will give you a good idea of where the attorney's philosophy lies. If the attorney discredits mediation, discourages resolving cases, talks about it as "weak" or "losing", you should choose another attorney.

On the other hand, while mediation is great, I have also encountered the philosophy that a person can go to mediation without an attorney. I realize that much of this book has been dedicated to discussing landmines in choosing an attorney and you may be asking, why get an attorney at all? Why not just go to mediation without attorneys? I discourage people from going to mediation without an attorney. You must understand that the mediator cannot give either party legal advice. The mediator's sole purpose is to get the parties to an agreement. The mediator cannot tell you if that agreement is fair under the law nor if you are negotiating away things that you would clearly be awarded if the case went to trial. The mediator cannot work to make sure you are protected or to prevent problems for you in the future.

Often people come to me after having been to mediation without an attorney. They realize they gave away things they never should have given away and they want me to fix it. Understand; it is very difficult to undo a settlement agreement. It will be very expensive to try to repair the mistakes the client made at mediation, and the likelihood of success is often low. Therefore, it makes much more sense to have an attorney help you from the beginning, ensure things are done properly the first time, and work to get you the best agreement possible at mediation while still protecting your interests.

7. *Will you explain the process to me?*
   If the attorney has not outlined the legal process already, you should ask him for an explanation. The response should be an easy to understand framework of the procedure. If the attorney is not willing to take the time necessary to educate you on what is going to happen and what your options are, then you should move on to a different attorney. Even though I have said those same things a million times, I want each client to understand the process. This is necessary so that I can set proper expectations for the client, and the client can be at ease knowing what will happen next and in what timeframe. The attorney should also outline an office procedure which includes the contact person for the client, a mechanism for communicating with that person and an office policy for how quickly emails or phone calls are returned. You should leave the attorney's office feeling like you have been educated and like you have been given a ton of information in a very short amount of time. You should not leave the attorney's office in a state of rage or with heightened emotions. The attorney should use the initial consultation to begin to train your logical mind to process information instead of inflaming your emotion. It is the first step to learning how to appropriately navigate a divorce.

8. *What technology do you use in the office?*
   As previously discussed, this inquiry helps you to determine if the attorney is focused on efficiency. Keep in mind
   that the more efficiently the attorney works, the less the
   case ultimately costs the client. For example, an office that
   uses an e-fax and scans case files instead of keeping a paper
   file has the capability to e-file documents. That means the
   client doesn't have to pay the attorney's assistant to drive
   down to the courthouse to file paperwork. There are many
   ways an attorney's efficiency saves the client money. I could
   spend pages giving examples. However, asking the question
   will let you know if this is the attorney's focus. Some attorneys do not care about being efficient. The more letters
   that are drafted and the more hands touch a document, the
   more the attorney is able to bill a client. The more billable
   time, the more money is charged. Therefore, some attorneys view an efficient office as contrary to the proverbial
   "bottom line."

9. *Will you reduce your hourly rate?*
   As much as you may not wish to hear this, the answer
   should be no. First, it is an accounting and billing night-
   mare to be working at different hourly rates for different
   clients. Beyond that, you do not want an attorney who
   doesn't value her time. If the attorney is so desperate for
   your case that she will bend the rules for you, then you
   need to move on. However, you should still ask the question. You want to see if the attorney will tell you no and
   how delicately she can answer the question. If the attorney
   becomes offended, you should move on. As a client you
   should be able to have an intellectual discussion on virtu-
   ally any topic with your attorney. Also, as the client, you
   want an attorney who is willing to tell you no. The greatest
   disservice an attorney can do for a client is to act as a

puppet. You are looking for an attorney who can logically and rationally take a position contrary to your wishes and explain the reasoning behind it in a way that makes sense to you. Requesting a lower rate is a good way to judge the attorney's ability to ultimately handle your case.

10. *Can you promise me _____ ?*

Often people enter my office and want a promise that if they pay me this money they will get X. ("X" could be majority timesharing, a certain amount of alimony, the marital residence, whatever the client is obsessing over at the time.) I give people this analogy: I happen to love football. I can watch tape, go over statistics, do research on injuries and so forth and put together a good presentation on what I think will happen during the game this weekend. But, I cannot promise you who will win. No one can make such a promise. There are too many moving parts and too many unknown variables. In many ways, a divorce (and a trial especially) is like football. It is a gamble. I can make an educated, researched, well-reasoned guess as to the eventual outcome, but I cannot make any promises.

The attorney may be tempted to make you promises. Maybe the attorney is so egotistical that he believes his actions can guarantee a certain outcome. There is no attorney that can really make such a promise, no matter how talented or experienced. In making such promises, these attorneys are being disingenuous. They either just want your retainer, or they are delusional. I understand the client is searching for certainty in the process. The client wants to know what will happen. However, you're going to have to let go of the need to predict the future. You have to choose an attorney using your logical mind, your Board of Directors and the tools of this book and trust that he is doing the best that can be done. The system doesn't always work swiftly and almost never along one certain path.

The closer you can get to an agreement with your spouse, the more control you have over your family and the more certain the divorce becomes. As you move from a place of love, you are better able to go with the flow and trust that your family will be brought through this process better in the end.

Your choice of an attorney is a really important factor in how your divorce will be decided and how effectively you will be able to save your family. Do not make that decision out of anger or haste. Use the initial consultation as an interview process. I encourage you to go to multiple attorneys to get a feel for the different styles and personalities. Never, ever hire an attorney because you feel pressure to move the case along. If you feel like you have to apologize for not hiring the attorney at the initial consultation, then you have not yet met the right attorney. An attorney who practices appropriately realizes this is a big decision and wants the client to be confident in her decision. Take the time to make an honest evaluation of the attorneys with whom you meet and make sure you are making your selection from a place of logic and reason.

The Anatomy of a Divorce

In the initial consultation, the attorney will need to get some background information from you. These are typically questions regarding the length of the marriage, financial status of the parties, children, assets, debts, etc. Once the attorney has all of the necessary information to give a general opinion on certain issues, he should then begin to tell you how the process works.

A divorce begins with a pleading filed with the court called a Petition for Dissolution of Marriage ("petition"). The petition outlines a skeletal picture of the history of the parties and the children involved. It also outlines the issues the party is asking the court to decide. For example, in addition to actually dissolving the marriage, the petition may ask the court to set a timesharing or visitation schedule with the children, to award child support, to award alimony, to divide debt, assets, houses and business interests, and award attorneys' fees. After the petition (and required accompanying documents) is filed, the other party may either accept service or have the papers delivered by a process server. Then opposing party has a certain number of days from the time the petition is served to file an answer. This time period is usually around twenty days but may vary depending on the circumstances.

After the answer is filed, the parties begin the process of exchanging documents to prepare the case. Most of these documents are finance-related and include verification of the exact nature and amount of all debts, assets and income. For example, the parties would exchange things like bank records, credit card statements, paystubs, mortgages, appraisals, etc. However, parties may generally ask for any item to be produced which the party thinks may lead to relevant information in the divorce and which the other party has in her possession. For relevant items not in the other party's possession, the attorney may issue a subpoena to third parties. Once financial information is compiled and the attorneys have a clear idea of the items to be distributed, the next step is to begin negotiations.

Many jurisdictions require parties to attend mediation. Sometimes the parties can get all issues resolved in mediation. Sometimes the parties are making progress at mediation but need additional documents or time to contemplate a proposed resolution so they will agree to come back for a second mediation. Sometimes the parties will see that they can come to agreement on some issues (timesharing) but cannot agree on others (alimony). If the parties agree on all issues, the case is basically over. The attorneys then prepare a Final Judgment for the Judge to sign which dissolves the marriage and makes your agreement an order of the Court resolving all issues.

If there are issues which are not agreed upon, a trial is set and the attorneys begin the process of preparing to present the client's case to the Judge. Each party will then ask the Judge to decide how the issue will be resolved. It generally takes a significant amount of time before the case is actually given a trial date. When you hear people complaining about a case taking forever, years and years, it is generally because the parties couldn't work out their differences and are waiting on a trial so the Judge can decide.

Once the Judge signs the Final Judgment, either after mediation or trial, the case is officially closed and the parties are free to go on about their lives and even re-marry if they are so inclined. The process can take 60 days or 600+ days. Where the case falls on the spectrum largely depends on the client and the attorney's motivation and perspective.

Keep in mind these are generalities. Every case is different and the specifics of your case can only be addressed with an attorney practicing in your State. After the attorney has explained exactly how a divorce process works logistically in your State and has given you an idea of the particular pleadings required for your case, the next step in the initial consultation is to review the contract.

The Attorney/Client Contract

As you engage the services of an attorney, you will be asked to sign a contract. I think it is prudent to go through what you can expect in the contract. I suppose I should say that if the attorney is not asking you to sign a contract, if the attorney just takes money and starts work, you probably have not made the best choice. I suggest you never hire an attorney without a contract.

As for the contract, expect there to be standard language, like any contract; that the agreement is the entire agreement, can be modified only in writing, etc. Really all contracts, whether for legal services or a major purchase, should have this language. The contract should also clearly define the services it includes. You are not, generally, hiring the attorney on retainer for all your needs forevermore. Consequently, the contract should clearly define the services included, as well as when the attorney's job is complete. For example, my divorce contracts clearly indicate the contract is complete upon signing the Final Judgment. Therefore, the client knows that anything after the divorce, like modification or contempt, is not covered under the initial divorce contract or retainer.

My divorce contracts also have the following provision:

Client's emotional family law case, counseling, and interventions.

Any family law case is not only a legal process but an emotional and psychological process for you, your spouse, and your family. If you are not already in counseling, you agree that you will begin and attend as recommended by the therapist. The length and expense of a legal case is usually affected by the emotional process. We find that the time and money spent in counseling is well spent. It not only assists you through the emotional process and coping with the stress in your professional and personal life caused by the divorce, but assists you in handling the legal process and coping with the stress of the case. If you are the initiator and are fully healed from the emotional process, counseling will help assist you in dealing with and communicating with your spouse in a different and more effective manner and in minimizing antagonism and anger to aid in amicable resolution.

If there are minor children, the client agrees to attend the court related mandatory four hour parenting course within thirty (30) days of this Contract. The class must be done in person and may not be completed through an online course. The education provided in this course includes the stages of dissolution of marriage, the impact of the dissolution on the parties, the children and the family, and skills related to eliminating conflict and the lessening the trauma of the dissolution of marriage. This immediate attendance is imperative to minimizing the fees and costs in the case. Failure to comply with this provision shall be grounds for the lawyer's withdrawal without further consent required from client.

If court action is necessary, the judge will look favorably on the client's retaining a therapist as well as a lawyer in assisting the client as it shows the client is educated as to the legal and emotional processes and desires to act responsibly and maturely with regards to the spouse and the family and amicably resolve matters and lessen legal fees and costs. The client will advise the lawyer of the name, address, and telephone number of the client's therapist and sign a release of information form with the lawyer. Other than this, all discussions with the therapist are confidential.

I find that this language is helpful as the attorney client relationship continues. When I am hearing emotional issues from the client, I can gently guide the client to this portion of the contract and suggest that, while the client's position is valid and should absolutely be addressed, perhaps it is better addressed in counseling where the client may actually be able to solve the problem. If the attorney has such language in the contract, it is a good indication the attorney truly understands the role of a Family Law attorney and can assist the client in the process of Divorcing with Joy.

The contract should also clearly outline the attorney's hourly rate as well as that of the paralegal and the other office staff. The attorney should have a clear procedure on how costs are handled. For example, what costs are absolutely required, such as the filing fee or mediation and what costs must be approved by the client prior to incurring, such as experts or private investigators. Never give the attorney unfettered access to spend your money on things the attorney believes are important for the case without a procedure for informing the client and getting client consent prior to spending the money.

The contract should also clearly outline the initial retainer. Sometimes initial retainers are non-refundable. It is a form of a minimum charge. Check to make sure your jurisdiction allows for non-refundable retainers. If permissible, they shouldn't scare you off so long as they are in line with what is generally charged in your area. The contract should also have an easily understandable provision for replenishing the retainer. The client should pay special attention to this provision. The quickest way to lose your attorney is to not pay them as required in the contract. It is not the attorney's job to chase the client for money and no attorney who is any good at his job will engage in such chase very long. Hopefully, if you're following the tenets of this book, the divorce will not become too costly and you will never have to avail yourself of the procedure to replenish the retainer. But, it is your job to plan and budget appropriately. The attorney is not a bank or a lending institution. It is a for-profit business and the attorney should run it as such.

Along that same line, the attorney should have a procedure for billing outlined in the contract. The client should know when to expect a bill, how long the client has to review the bill, and the office policy on charging the client for things like postage, copies, etc. All of these things should be clearly defined in the contract. Often attorneys are not known for sending statements timely or regularly. The problem when the attorneys aren't diligent about submitting statements every month is that the client's bill can get completely out of control before the client even realizes it. In every attorney's office, sometimes things fall through the crack. However, if you have a provision in the contract telling you when to expect the statement and then you don't receive it, you know to call or email the attorney to follow up. Often it is just an oversight, especially if you have always received a statement in the past or if it is your first statement. Even if you don't owe money, the attorney should send a statement and you should insist on receiving it. These statements will give you an idea of where your retainer money is being used and you then have the opportunity to make adjustments if necessary.

Lastly, the contract should have a clearly defined "rights and responsibilities of the lawyer and client" clause. In my contract, such provision is as follows:

Rights and responsibilities of the lawyer and the client.

a. The client agrees to follow the advice and recommendations of the lawyer.

b. The client agrees to tell the lawyer the truth, to keep the lawyer advised of changes in address, telephone numbers, and e-mail addresses, to cooperate in the preparation and trial of the case, to appear on reasonable notice for negotiations, mediations, depositions, and court appearances, to comply with all reasonable requests made of the client in connection with preparation and presentation of the case.

c. The client understands that it is office practice to compute not less than one-tenth of an hour for each telephone call, e-mail, or fax, no matter how short its duration or duration of review, and such additional time as may actually be expended, whether the telephone calls, e-mails, or faxes, are from or to the client or others concerning the case. Therefore, the client agrees to keep notes and consolidate inquiries and meetings to minimize fees and costs.

d. The lawyer agrees to keep the client informed of the status of his or her case.

e. The lawyer agrees not to settle or compromise the client's claims without discussing the matter with and obtaining the prior agreement of the client. The client agrees not to settle or compromise the client's claims without discussing the matter with and obtaining the prior agreement of the lawyer.

f. *It is the client's right to receive copies of all important papers prepared on the client's behalf or received from the court or the other side. The client agrees to contact the lawyer to explain any papers the client does not understand.*

Termination of Services.

In addition to the provisions set forth elsewhere in this Contract, the client has a right to terminate representation by the lawyer at any time for no cause and the lawyer has a right to terminate representation of the client at any time for no cause. The lawyer maintains a right to terminate representation immediately if the client fails to tell the truth, misrepresents or fails to disclose a material fact to the lawyer, fails to follow the lawyer's advice, fails to make payments as required by this Contract, or demands that the lawyer do something unlawful or unethical.

This informs the client of exactly what the attorney will or will not do for the client and sets some appropriate boundaries. The client should know that the attorney is not engaged in the business of misrepresenting facts to the Court and the attorney will not tolerate the client misrepresenting facts to the attorney. In the end, it doesn't serve anyone well in the legal process.

If there are things in the contract that you do not understand, don't be hesitant to ask the attorney about the contract. If the attorney is at all impatient or offended, you have not chosen the right attorney. You also have the absolute right to have another attorney review the contract before you sign it. Some of my clients have engaged an attorney to review the contract prior to their signature, and it doesn't bother me at all. I appreciate that clients understand the gravity of what they are about to sign and want to make an informed choice.

PRACTICAL APPLICATION OF REASON OVER EMOTION

Legal Divorce vs. Emotional Divorce

NOW that you are ready to move forward with divorce, there is a very particular way in which the divorce process is best handled. If you have chosen an attorney well, the attorney will help you reign in emotions and use the legal system most efficiently, in the way it was designed to be used. But, it is not easy to keep the divorce about logic and reason. It is possible, now that you are well into the process of working on yourself, but still it is not easy.

How many times in your life have you looked back on a fight you had with someone and thought to yourself, "My goodness, that was a waste. Why was I fighting about that?" Almost always, right? Very few fights in life are reflected upon years later and determined to be a good decision. This is because most fights are emotional. When the emotion is removed (often years later) the fight no longer makes any sense. The trick in a divorce is to get to that place in the beginning thereby preventing the unnecessary fight and, by extension, the unnecessary damage to you and your family. It is to see the fight prospectively as wasteful and emotionally driven as opposed to only being able to have such perspective years later, upon reflection.

There are two very distinct aspects of a divorce: the emotional component and the legal component. Generally speaking, the legal component of a divorce is not that complicated. On the vast majority of cases, you can present the facts to three or four experienced Family

Law attorneys and they will give you a good estimate of what will happen in the case. There are exceptions and sometimes complex legal issues if, for example, the married couple owns significant assets or multiple businesses. But these are just that, the exceptions.

I recently heard a Judge speaking of attorneys. The Judge reinforced some points I believe to be absolutely true. The Judge described a successful Family Law practice as one in which 85% to 90% of the cases settle without going to trial. The remaining percentage goes to trial because there is a genuine legal issue or a truly unreasonable opposing party over whom the attorney has no control. The Judge also indicated that Judges know the attorneys who aren't practicing appropriately because those attorneys are the ones always in trial. Judges see a small percentage of attorneys over and over again in trials. The intimation was that Judges lose respect for the attorneys who go to trial frequently on Family Law cases. Respect, both from the client and the judiciary, is something that every attorney needs in order to serve the client's best interest.

Be aware that Judges are always looking for the party in a divorce who is acting out of emotion. Judges expect there to be a certain amount of emotion in a divorce. However, they also expect the attorney to manage that emotion and keep the proceedings in court as rational and logical as possible. A client does not want to be labeled the "emotional" one in a divorce. With such a label, there is a danger the Judge will stop listening to the client's points, even the valid ones, and prejudge her positions as emotionally driven instead of logic based. Once a client acquires such a label it becomes monumentally more difficult to achieve the ideal result from the Judge.

There is a simple explanation for why divorces are so expensive and why are there so many very wealthy divorce attorneys. The fact is that people will spend their retirement, their children's future college fund or their inheritance attempting, in vain, to get an emotional resolution in the legal system. The basic problem is that people confuse the two aspects of the divorce. They erroneously attach an emotional component to a legal issue. They want to feel vindicated and made whole by the Judge. It is a "That son of a bitch cheated on me and now I am going to make him pay" sort of mentality.

Well, here is the issue. The Judge doesn't care that he cheated on you. People cheat on their spouses every single day, and the Judge sees it every single day. It doesn't offend her sense of basic justice. Even if it did, Judges are trained to apply the law with an even hand, impartially and without emotion. So, when a client attempts to get the judge to "make it right", to punish the spouse, the client ends up spending a lot of emotional and monetary currency without reward.

Often people are acting out their emotions in the legal components of a divorce without even realizing it. They won't come out and say a phrase as blatant as the one above, but that is the underlying current or reason behind the thought or behavior. Just because something is logically reasoned doesn't mean it isn't emotionally driven. I have seen many examples in the course of my practice. People who are frustrated with the process, are having trouble letting go or are on a crusade for justice are emotionally driven. Clients are happier with the process when they are able to see these feelings as emotional responses to legal problems.

Frustration

If you are frustrated, it is your fault. People really hate it when I tell them these things. It frustrates them. But, it is absolutely true. If you have an opinion on something or on how the case is going, express that opinion. Receive the person's reaction and make a calculated next move. The outcome, however, cannot be predicted or controlled. For example, often people come to me "frustrated" because the case isn't moving along fast enough. The greatest response to this is, "Why?" Unfortunately, court systems are clogged. This is especially true since the collapse of the housing market. Home prices fell and the government is collecting much less in property taxes. This has a trickle-down effect on all levels of government, including the court system. Locally, retiring Judges aren't being replaced and divisions are left vacant. This means that nothing in court happens quickly and, if people want a quick solution, they need to learn to resolve their own differences.

When people express "frustration" that the case isn't over quickly enough, I challenge their thought process. What "emotions" are you having that require relief? Why are you expecting the finalization of the divorce to relieve this emotion? If you are frustrated with the process, then you have more work to do on your perspective. I spend a good portion of my life listening to people. The frustration I hear most often is with the spouse. I hear people in great angst and frustration that the spouse is spending money recklessly, spoiling the kids, sending nasty emails, etc. I ask the client if this is new behavior. The client always says, "No, he has been doing this the whole marriage." Then why in the world would you expect him to behave any differently in the process of a separation/divorce? It is insanity to do the same thing over and over and expect a different result. It is equally insane to be frustrated with spouses for being as they have always been. You should expect the same behavior and be pleasantly surprised if your spouse begins to behave differently. There should be no frustration involved.

It doesn't mean the spouse's actions are appropriate. There may be a mechanism in the legal system to address the grievance and, if so, an attorney will give you the legal options moving forward. You can weigh them and pick one. But, often there aren't good legal remedies. In that scenario, your attorney should explore some creative problem solving. Call on your common sense to see what might actually work going forward. Maybe, in the end, the only thing you can change is how you view the situation. Don't see this as a defeat. It is truly the most powerful of abilities. No matter where your issue falls, it shouldn't be frustrating. When you feel frustration in the process, I encourage you to explore the reasons behind the frustration. It is almost always an emotional reaction. When you are in a good place mentally, emotionally, and spiritually, almost nothing is frustrating. The same is true in the divorce process. When you are taking care of you and allow other people to have their path through the process, there is no frustration. It just is.

A Child of Divorce

To share some personal experience with divorces in which emotion ruled over logic and reason, I share with you my experiences as a child of divorce. My own actual legal divorce was easy. All the hard work was before and after (we will discuss the "after" as the last portion of this book). My parents' divorce was nasty. My Mother was cheating on my Father. She was having an affair with an elder in the church. After evening church, she would leave my sister (who was two at the time) with me (I was four) in the car in the church parking lot while she went away with him. I remember it seemed like hours we were in that parking lot. It was very dark and I remember being very scared. Then we'd get home and my parents would fight. There was a lot of yelling. Shortly thereafter they divorced.

I know way too much about their divorce. I was young and all I should've been told was that both of my parents loved me very much and we would always be a family even if we didn't always live in the same house. What I actually know is that my Mother left and took everything out of the house down to the nails out of the walls and the toilet seats off the toilets. At the time, I remember feeling like we were robbed somehow. I remember seeing the only home I'd ever known so bare that I felt violated and unsafe. My Mother was very hurt and vengeful throughout the divorce. She wanted money and lots of it. She accused my Father of being controlling during the marriage. My Father was very angry. He had a hard time controlling his emotions when interacting with my Mother. The fighting between the two of them was incessant. We were brought into the middle of the divorce and I remember being told all the problems of the marriage back then.

It is a very difficult struggle for a child to be thrown into the problems leading to a divorce. My Mother would show me the child support check written by my Father. She would tell me that if my Father loved me, he would pay more support. Every time we were exchanged for timesharing with the other parent it was tense and uncomfortable. I remember the two of them yelling at each other on the phone every time they spoke. I remember telling my Mother that it made sense that we stay a week with her and a week with Daddy. She went into a fit of rage and made me swear never to say that to my Father because if I did he would "take me away from her." She would become so agitated that it was not unusual for her to slap me in the face. We were often treated as possessions rather than people.

Now, looking back on it with my lifetime of experiences, I see things much differently than I did as a child. I see that my Mother was acting out of fear. She was afraid that she would "lose" us. She was afraid she wouldn't be financially stable on her own. She was acting out of emotion. My Father had his idea of what was right, and he was sticking to that no matter what. He didn't believe it was right that my Mother received any more than the minimum financially because she was irresponsible with money and because she cheated on him. They both were acting out of emotion. If they weren't, they never would have fought in front of us the way they did. Emotion causes people to do things that don't make sense. It made no sense to subject a child to that kind of environment. The closer they got to the actual trial, the more the atmosphere deteriorated. I don't know what was said in that trial but I know that my parents continued to fight for years to come. Whatever happened in that courtroom, it wasn't good and it wasn't healing.

The Parent Who Just Can't Let Go

Having been through a divorce, I understand the fear of letting go. I recall early in the separation process, when I was trying to figure things out, I obsessed about "losing" my kids. All I could think about was the time I would miss. I couldn't imagine not being there to hug them in the morning or kiss them goodnight. It was the first time in ten years I wasn't in a couple and I felt lonely. From this place of loneliness, it terrified me that I would not have my kids. I was not comfortable in my own skin and could not imagine being in the house all alone. I was clinging to them to fill the hole left by the breakdown of my marriage.

As I said earlier, there was a time initially when I was with the boys nearly 100% of the time and I was able to see the negative effects on the boys when they are without their Father. So, I had to find a way to let go of my fear of being alone. I found the more I worked with my Board of Directors, the easier it was to adjust to an empty house. As I found things I enjoyed and became comfortable in the stillness, I began to value my time without the boys. I believe my ex-husband is a better Father without me there to divide his attention. We can each be completely focused on the boys during our time with them. I use my time alone to refocus and regroup. As it turns out, the boys are much better for it and they have more balanced, well-adjusted parents.

However, I see the fear of letting go in my practice often. It is a terrifying proposition, especially for a parent who has been primarily responsible for caring for the children, to relinquish any amount of control and responsibility to the other parent. Many states have moved to a system in which equal timesharing is favored. Often people have a strong reaction to the possibility that they may "lose" their children half the time. Understand that even the phrasing of this concept is emotional. Time your children spend with the other parent is not time "lost" from you no more than time spent with you is time "lost" from the other parent. Parents who begin a case from this mindset do not have the ability to think rationally.

The most extreme (although not at all uncommon) example of this type of behavior is found in cases where a parent makes an unfounded allegation of abuse against the other parent. A parent will say that the spouse verbally, mentally or sexually abused her or the children. Sometimes parents will even coach the children to make the same allegation. At that point, the Court has to intervene and act in an abundance of caution. Next the judge orders supervised visitation, often through a court supervised program. Because of the number of cases, the visitations often only occur for a few hours, a couple of times a month. The facility closely monitors the visitation, in a very sterile room, and often doesn't allow the parent and child to even touch. As you can imagine, this is a huge shock to the children. They feel as though they are visiting a "bad" parent who has done something wrong.

It is very confusing for a child to transition from a traditional family relationship to a situation where they are having supervised visits with a parent. Remember, the child internalizes each thing said about the other parent. Therefore, the child begins to wonder what she did wrong to warrant such a drastic change. The child misses the parent, feels alienated and is confused. Supervised visitation should be reserved for only the most extreme cases of child abuse or endangerment. I believe that the parent making the accusation often doesn't understand the wheels that will be put in motion once the allegation is made. I think the parent is blinded by the overwhelming panic (i.e. emotion) at the thought of "losing" her child half the time, will do almost anything to alleviate the panic and is not thinking logically. Or worse, an attorney has hinted that the parent can have timesharing, child support and alimony addressed in an injunction against domestic violence prior to filing the divorce and that, if there were such an injunction, she would have the upper hand in the divorce. The parent believes she can gain an advantage and control over the situation, then "take it back" later. However, it just doesn't work that way. Once such allegations are made the Court has a responsibility to protect the children. A parent who makes such allegations can never go back and say it isn't true because such a confession would indicate parental alienation and greatly affect the ultimate visitation schedule awarded. So begins a very vicious cycle that is monumentally harmful to the children.

It may sound like an extreme situation but, really, it is far too common. Often people will act out of character in the beginning stages of a divorce. Let's say, for example, a Husband has caught the Wife in the act of cheating. In a fit of rage, he throws the Wife against the wall and punches the man. Now, this would tend to show the Husband is violent and can certainly be the basis for a domestic violence injunction. The Wife could also use this as a basis to ask the Court for supervised visitation for the children. The Husband is violent, out of control, etc. However, if the Husband never before displayed any violence toward the children, is a request for supervised visitation, while legally permissible, really in their best interests? It may be tempting to use the Husband's mistake to "take the screws to him" in the divorce, but be cautious of great danger when such a decision is made from a place of anger and hurt emotion rather than logically what is best for the children. There are less extreme examples such as a Wife keying the Husband's car and threatening to kill him if he ever _____ again or a parent throwing something in the course of an argument and accidently hitting the spouse or even one of the kids, etc.

While violence is never good and should not be condoned, I encourage you to see two ways of approaching the situation. One, look at it from a place of grace. Ultimately, is the offending parent a good person and parent? If the answer is yes, seek creative solutions to ensure the safety of the children, maximize their contact with the other parent, and encourage as normal a relationship as possible while still protecting everyone involved. Or two, see it as an opportunity to get revenge, act out of anger, hurt the other parent and thereby the children. The second approach may be tempting and may even feel good at the time. A client can reason the decision by saying that the client is only acting to protect the children. The client can even portray herself as a martyr who is giving up a normal life and taking on 100% responsibility for the children because the spouse is a horrible, violent person. The law may even allow this to happen. However, just because the decision is reasoned doesn't mean it isn't emotionally driven. Always be aware that there may be other, well-reasoned alternatives that do not make one parent a victim and the other a demon. Choose an option from a place of grace and love and your children will be happier and healthier for it.

The Person on a Crusade for Justice

There are a couple of common misperceptions that deserve some attention. First, people believe Family Law is about justice. It is not. At least it is not about your idea of justice. It is about what is in the best interest of the children. It is about taking one family unit and making it two family units in a way that is in line with the law and makes the most sense for the collective whole. Second, women are more likely to portray themselves as victims. This is equally untrue. Men and women sometimes manifest victimization differently, but one is no more prevalent than the other. These two misconceptions are variants of a single mentality: victim mode.

Most states are no fault states. All the courts require is one person to testify the marriage is irretrievably broken. It doesn't matter what happened. The Judge doesn't care. Work that out in therapy, not the legal system. Too often people want to vent in court thinking they will get some kind of vindication. This is a waste of money, time and resources. You may have been seriously wronged in your marriage. But, replaying yourself as the victim over and over in the context of the legal system isn't going to change the fact that you were wronged. It is only going to make the scar from the hurt more permanent. Because the divorce process isn't going to deliver the "justice" you desire, you are then going to blame the system. You are going to say that the system is broken, unfair, uncaring, unjust, and then you become the victim of your spouse and the system. There is a way of moving forward that is the opposite of the victim mode. It is, essentially, full of grace. Here is an example of the contrast between the two.

Wife separates from her Husband after thirty years of marriage and three minor kids. She finds out that her Husband is, in fact, homosexual and engaged in affairs with men during the marriage. The most recent affair was ongoing. Her Husband also had issues with alcohol, probably exacerbated by his double lifestyle. There are two very distinct ways of handling the situation. A) The Wife is angry, wants to lash out at the spouse, wants him to have no visitation, pay all the marital debt because he was probably spending it on his boyfriends anyway, wants spousal support, and "deserves the marital home because he promised it to me." Or B) The Wife is very hurt and tearful but admits that her Husband was a good Dad, that the children love him. She wants to formulate a parenting plan that ensures the children's safety but which also maximizes time with Dad. The client wants to equally divide all the assets and liabilities and wants to move on.

Wife A is very much in victim mode. Was she wronged? Absolutely. Does drawing out a long divorce battle change the fact that she was wronged? No. Is she going to get everything she wants in the divorce because it wasn't her fault that her Husband turned out to be gay and cheated on her for decades? Nope. Is she going to feel any better after the divorce is over, the Judge has heard all of the proverbial "dirty laundry" and makes a decision? She isn't. Anything short of getting everything she wants is going to be perceived as a "loss" in her mind. The Judge isn't going to put any weight whatsoever in his affairs or sexual orientation. Ultimately, her divorce will be a horrible experience. She will hate her attorney, the Judge and her ex-husband. She will be as miserable divorced as she was married.

Now, to the contrary, client B comes into the divorce with very realistic expectations. She is extending a good amount of grace to her Husband. Yes, he has made mistakes. Yes, those mistakes are very hurtful to her. However, she is focusing not on her hurt and anger but on the positive things about him. You cannot be married for any length of time to a person who is devoid of good qualities. At some point, you saw something good in the other person. Now is the time to focus on those good qualities, as difficult as it may be. Wife B came into the divorce no less hurt, but with a very different mindset. She wasn't going to allow the hurt and pain to perpetuate more hurt and pain.

Instead of focusing on the negative and giving energy to the hurt, she focused on the positive qualities of her spouse and devised a plan to maximize those good qualities for the benefit of the children. She didn't try to punish him for what he'd done and she didn't try to use the divorce to ruin his life. Did he deserve this? Well, no. But that's not the point. Every single person needs grace sometimes. We all make mistakes, we need someone to see the good in us and see beyond our bad behavior. We never "deserve" grace. That's the whole point. If you deserved it you wouldn't need it. Grace is not for the perfect but the imperfect. Who benefited most from her grace? Not her spouse. The people who benefited most from her grace were her children. Client B understands this instinctively. Her children maintained a relationship with their Father and the parents continued as a family unit. After processing the hurt and anger, the client was able to move on to a happier and healthier life, filled with positivity and love.

Wife B spends minimal money on the divorce which takes only a few months from start to finish. Wife A exhausts much of the marital assets, engages in a legal battle for years and suffers great emotional turmoil and hurt as a result of her victim mindset. With the same basic facts, the process can go either very well or very poorly. The difference is only this: the perspective of the Wife. Wife B did her work before making a decision on the future of the marriage.

She processed her feelings about the separation and didn't jump forward to divorce out of hurt, anger or fear. In the end, although she decides to move forward with a divorce, it is a productive, therapeutic process that allows the family to be healthier moving forward.

Women do not have a monopoly on operating in victim mode. Men portray themselves as the "victims" in divorces just as often. Usually, a man in victim mode is linked to his sense of right and wrong, a quest for justice. Often women present themselves as the victim emotionally. They are more likely to offer these complaints: *He was disconnected. I didn't feel loved. All he ever did was work. He's abandoning me.* (I could go on for a few pages, but I think you get the idea.) Men often present themselves as the victim of what they perceive as an unfair system. Men are more likely to complain about being *taken to the cleaners.* I hear men talk more often about not wanting to get "screwed" financially. *I don't want this divorce. It's not right that I pay alimony.* They complain that the woman didn't earn any of the money, why then should she get a check every month? *I earned that 401(K), why should I have to lose half of it? It's just not right.*

Frequently, when people sit in front of me and tell me the story of their marriage or what they expect to get at the end of the divorce, the conversation goes directly to "right" or "wrong". First of all, I should point out that what is "right" or "wrong" is very subjective. Often your sense of what is right and your spouse's sense of what is right are polar opposites. Your spouse could think it is "right" that you never see the kids because you were checked out during the marriage, and your spouse was the parent primarily responsible for caretaking of the children. There are two diametrically opposite ideas of justice for every issue and usually there is a spouse planted firmly on each side. Therefore, if the system factored in either party's sense of justice it would often cancel out anyway. It doesn't mean either party's sense of right and wrong is flawed, it just means each has a different perspective.

Inevitably when the client begins talking about right and

wrong, my response in my head is "What does that have to go with anything?" What I actually say is something like this, "I understand you feel X is right and Y is wrong. However, here is what the law says. The law has nothing to do with what you think is right or wrong." Then, people become disenfranchised with the system. *The system sucks. The law isn't fair. I'm getting screwed.* Understand that, no matter how much you dislike it, your attorney cannot go into court and say, "Yes, your honor, I understand what the law requires. However, the law is different than my client's sense of what is right; therefore, I object." See how silly it is?

When a client is on a never-ending quest for his version of justice, it is almost always an emotional reaction. If you say it a different way, it is easy to see. What the client is really saying is, "I don't feel like that is right." You remember the line from A League of Their Own, "There is no crying in baseball." Well, there is no feeling in the legal system. What you feel is right doesn't matter. What you feel is wrong doesn't matter. These are emotions, and to get through the legal process of divorce most effectively, you have to separate feelings from your legal case. You have to separate emotion from the law. The law is the application of a set of rules to a set of facts. Nowhere, in the equation appears any one person's belief of right or wrong. It just is. You are not a victim of the legal system because you don't like the way the law applies to your set of facts. As long as you walk through the case in victim mode, you will be unhappy.

Impossible to Please

Another example of an emotionally driven client is the person who is impossible to please. The glaring truth is that, at some point in a divorce, the client is going to have to cut her losses. The best divorces are ones where the spouses get what they can and get out. However, some clients get so entrenched in their idea of justice that they simply cannot give things up. The most extreme example of this type of this mindset is the case in which people fight over personal possessions. I have literally witnessed fighting over extension cords. Clearly, fighting over personal possessions is almost always an emotional decision, but people simply don't see it at the time. *That's my sword collection. That's my painting. I want it.* When a client is spending $300 per hour fighting over furniture or a mattress or cologne or tools or (insert whatever item seems so important at the time), it is never about the thing.

Clients get in the mindset that it isn't "right" that she keep, for example, the tools. After all, she doesn't even know how to use them. *It isn't right that she took $250 of my cologne; she is just going to give it to her new boyfriend.* And, truly, these things may not be "right". Maybe the other person will snicker all the way to the boyfriend's house to give him the cologne. But, really, so what? Trust me, with that mindset she will end up just as unhappy with the new boyfriend as she was with her Husband. If these types of things bother a client so much that he wants to fight about it in a divorce, he is clearly not using a logical mind. Logically, it makes no sense to spend exponentially more money fighting about the item than the item is worth. If ever a client encounters an attorney who doesn't explain what a financially irresponsible decision such a fight is, the client should be aware that the attorney is just out to make money and should not be a trusted advisor. An attorney who advises a client to let this go is not a pushover or weak, the attorney is just looking out for the client's interest while he is living in an irrational state of mind.

A person who is acting out of emotion and can never be pleased is also the one who keeps moving the ball. This client engages in endless negotiation. Initially, he may come to the attorney with a list of five things he wants out of the divorce. The attorney then works very diligently to get those things and manages to get very, very close. Then the client adds five more things that are suddenly deal breakers. The real issue is that the client doesn't want to get divorced. Always be aware that sometimes the natural tendency is to extend conflict. At least if the conflict is extended, there is some sort of relationship between the parties. The client doesn't have to face the fact that he is "divorced" or that his spouse may move on to another relationship. He may not even realize he is doing this. Sometimes I see an enormous amount of tension in clients at the mere mention of signing an agreement to resolve all the issues of the divorce. The client becomes afraid he is getting "screwed" and develops great anxiety that the marriage is about to be over. These feelings have nothing to do with what is on the paper or the terms of the agreement. It is, exclusively, an emotional reaction.

Often clients can't identify the emotion, however. They keep negotiating, adding terms, adding "deal-breakers" and keep going and going and going. Such client is completely out of his logical mind and into his emotional mind. This is true even if there are some seemingly logical thoughts behind the continued requests. I have had many conversations with clients in which I have told them to just stop. The conversation usually goes something like this, "You asked for x, y, and z. I got you x, y and z. Then you asked for a, b, and c. I got you a and c. Now you want to fight about b and add in e, f, and g. I need for you to really think about what this is worth to you because you are going to spend thousands and thousands of dollars fighting for these things when I have gotten you 80% of what you asked, and in that fight before the Judge, you may very well lose some of those things." The conversation is designed to get the client out of emotion and into logic. I imagine that 20% seems huge for him and it is all in the world the client can focus on. Taking emotion out of it, is it really worth the fight? The answer is usually no.

However, many attorneys won't have this conversation. Notice what is happening for the attorney. In having this conversation, the attorney is encouraging the resolution in which the attorney makes the least amount of money. I believe, as many attorneys do, that we have an ethical and moral obligation to have this conversation with the client. However, ultimately, it is up to the client to be vigilant that he is always making decisions from a place of logic.

Money, Money, Money, Money

Often an emotionally driven decision in a divorce stems around paying support. I routinely hear parents complain about paying support (alimony or child support) because the other spouse is so irresponsible with money. *I want to make sure she doesn't spend the money on alcohol or spa appointments or cigarettes. I want to make sure the money goes toward the children.* First, imagine a situation in which you are monitoring every expense paid from child support from here forward. Do you really want to be that tied up with your ex for the next decade or longer? And, what if the roles were reversed? What if your spouse said, "I am going to judge how much you can pay based on your spending habits and I am going to catalogue every dime you spend?" How would you like it?

Know that when you are having these types of feelings about paying support, it is an emotionally driven decision. Yes, you can reasonably say that your spouse is terrible with money and tends to make bad financial decisions. However, that is no reason to spend thousands of dollars to fight about support. To do so, makes you the financially irresponsible party. Most states have formulas to determine child support. It just is what it is. Don't ever, ever fight for custody only because you want to pay less child support. Even if you don't trust your spouse with money, pay a reasonable amount of support and move on. If there ever is a time in which the children are not being cared for properly, then you will have some ammunition to ask the Court to modify the visitation schedule and child support. But, this is one of those situations where you have to give spouses some rope and see if they hang themselves. Do not begrudge any money paid for support, for ultimately, it is done as an act of love for your children regardless of the choice the other parent makes in how to spend it.

Conversely, if you are on the receiving end of support, be respectful. Don't flaunt irresponsible financial decisions and say you used child support to fund them. I encourage families to exchange support through an order such that the money is removed from the payor's paycheck prior to receipt. This way, it is never late and the parties never have to talk about it. It significantly reduces the tension around the subject.

People often attach a "right" or "wrong" to child support. I hear *It isn't right that he not support his children* or *It isn't right that she gets one-third of my paycheck*. Recognize these as emotional reactions. When my Husband and I separated, he was in a precarious financial position. It took him a few months to find a job and even longer to rebuild an independent life. As a result, I did not ask him for child support for quite some time. Was it "right" that he not pay child support? I don't know. But, I figured the best thing he could do for our children was to be financially secure. If I took support from him, it would delay the rebuilding of his new life. I didn't want the boys to see their Father struggling and in financial ruin. So, I didn't press the issue. Relatively quickly, he was able to set himself up in an apartment where the boys had their own room, a community pool and a playground. It was good for them and his half of the family unit. I could see no logic in taking child support and delaying this transition. Once he was re-established, I never had to fight him to get child support. I receive it every two weeks like clockwork.

Handling the situation from a place of grace instead of entitlement was best for our family as a whole. I could have made him pay all along and fought with him about it. I could have said that it wasn't right. I could have called him a deadbeat. I could have seen myself as the "victim" because he wasn't paying and I was carrying the financial load myself. Those are all unproductive emotions. He was not a villain. He was a newly single Father trying to rebuild. I was not a victim. I could take care of our boys without child support. When emotions were set aside and consideration was given to the family, the collective whole, it just made sense.

Emotion almost always surrounds alimony. If you have a

situation where 2 out of 3 attorneys tell you that you are going to be paying alimony, find a way to live with that fact. Attorneys make a great living on people who don't want to pay alimony or who want to receive an exorbitant amount of alimony. It is, without a doubt, one of the most emotionally driven aspects of a divorce. It is the "she doesn't deserve to get paid just because she was married to me" or, "I am going to hurt his wallet because he hurt me" mentality. If you find yourself in such a situation, I encourage you to look at the situation from your spouse's perspective. Understand his fears and concerns and come to a reasonable resolution. You may not be totally comfortable with the outcome, but at least it is one over which you exercised some control. It is almost always an emotional decision when you start to "starve" your spouse out, allow the electricity to be disconnected, or create other financial disasters just to keep from paying support. Although it may be very difficult, use great effort to make a logical decision regarding support void of emotion, anger and resentment.

The number of examples available to illustrate how a person can get caught up in emotion as opposed to logic and reason in the course of a divorce is endless. Literally, every decision can be swayed or influenced by emotion. There are many different ways to handle each situation and each falls somewhere on the spectrum between purely emotional at one end and purely logical at the other. Take care not to be fooled into believing that your decision is logical just because there are reasons to justify it. Always put yourself in the other person's shoes and use every effort to see both sides of the issue. If you are unable to see both sides, choose an attorney who will illustrate both sides for you. Don't reject a proposed solution just because you initially find it uncomfortable. If you are acting from a place of emotion, a rational, logical solution will seem very uncomfortable. As you continue through the process of Divorcing with Joy, you will find it easier and easier to make decisions in the legal case absent emotion. As you become happy, you become more forgiving and better able to act appropriately. Even if you don't see yourself there now, you will get there. In the meantime, surround yourself with people you trust and do the best that you can.

10 THINGS TO NEVER DO IN A DIVORCE

IN the course of a divorce, both attorneys and Judges are always on guard for people who have not yet gained the ability to think rationally, but rather, are acting purely out of emotion. "Off the record" we would say we are looking for the crazy one. While there are very few absolutes in this world and even less in the context of a divorce, there are some red flags. If you find yourself tempted to do any one of these things, I would encourage you to really check your motives because they are almost always an emotional reaction.

1. Never deny contact between your spouse and the children without first talking to several attorneys and hiring representation (unless you have a court order of no contact such as through an injunction or restraining order). While you may hate your spouse so much that you want to punish her and you may not trust her at all, you must work hard to maintain a relationship between the other parent and child. Even if she is so caught up in emotion that she doesn't seem to care, it is your job for your children's sake to make that relationship happen. Your children will appreciate this from you as they get older. Plus, once you have literally done everything possible to normalize the relationship, your kids cannot be resentful of you later in life for "taking Mommy away." It will, clearly, never be you who thwarted the relationship in any way. Lastly, if the case goes to trial, the Judge will look favorably upon

you for your ability to place your children's best interest above your emotional process. Judges want the children to be entrusted to the parent who is most likely to facilitate a loving and nurturing relationship with the other parent. Your acts of grace in working to maintain a relationship between your spouse and the children will serve you well in life and in the divorce. It is not always easy and sometimes it feels as though you are swallowing a lot of pride to make it happen. It takes great strength to work for a healthy relationship between your spouse and your children when, truly, you are not feeling it. It will, however, be worth it.

2. Never say anything negative about the other parent in front of the children. Also, always watch your body language when you are around the other parent. Children pick up on these things. It cannot be stressed enough that everything, good or bad, said about the other parent is internalized by the child such that the child will believe that thing about him. As much as you may choke on the words, lift up the other parent for your child. Say nice things about him and pretend like you mean it. The children will then know that the divorce is not their fault, it is okay to love the both parents and things will ultimately be okay.

    Know that the "rock" in the children's lives has always been your marriage. They feel as though they are now going through an earthquake and there is a crack in the foundation of their lives. The more you lift up the other parent for them, the safer the children feel and the quicker they will adjust. Don't do it because the other parent "deserves" it. Do it because your children deserve it. The Judge will respect your ability to continue to praise the other parent. It will be refreshing for the Judge because they don't see that type of thing nearly as often as they should.

3. Never record the other party without her permission. It, truly, just makes you look crazy. Don't bring out topless pictures your Wife sent you or sex tapes or anything else you think may be "blackmail". I could tell you horror stories of people who walked around with tape recorders documenting arguments or, worse, who put surveillance in the car or home to record the other parent having sex outside the marriage. Clients then think they have some "trump" card and want to use this "evidence" in court. While there are some rare instances where this might be relevant, those are few and far between. And, if you are so entrenched in the emotions of the case that you are getting surveillance on your spouse, chances are that you are not acting rationally.

I have even seen cases where the parent played these surveillance tapes for the children. Never, ever do that. The parent insisted the children know what happened so that they knew where to place the blame for the breakdown of the marriage. It is none of the children's concern why the marriage didn't work. Resist the urge to create a demon and a victim for the children. This is true whether the children are sixteen or six. When the Judge discovers you subjected the children to this type of behavior, the Judge is not going to like it and you will have seriously damaged your case.

4. Never refuse to financially support your children. I don't care if your spouse gets her nails done every week or if he just bought a new Harley. Regardless how the other parent spends his money, you have an obligation to support your child. Because the formula for child support incorporates the visitation schedule, if the court gets the idea a

parent doesn't want to pay child support, the Court may think any request for custody or additional timesharing is just to avoid paying child support. This could seriously damage the legal case and invalidate any request for custody. Additionally, if a parent is financially supporting the child throughout the case, it prevents a huge amount of support accumulating that the Judge could order in one big payment at the end of the case.

5. Never send nasty emails, text messages, letters or voicemails to your spouse. It is normal to get angry at times in the course of a divorce. Much like in a criminal case, anything you say or do can be used against you in court. Please have the ability to remain silent. Write in a journal, go to therapy, hit some golf balls, take up boxing, or go have drinks with a trusted friend but do not vent to the spouse. Maturity is paramount. Disengage and, eventually, when the spouse realizes you are not going to fight, the bad behavior will fizzle. How fun is it, after all, to fight with yourself?

6. Never fire an attorney because the attorney isn't saying what you want to hear. Keep in mind that one huge red flag for attorneys and Judges is the client who has been through a number of attorneys. When a client has had multiple attorneys representing him, the Judge will assume he cannot listen to reason. Even if a client is having issues with the attorney, those issues should be addressed directly with the attorney in a logical and rational way. The client should honestly evaluate the motives behind the dissatisfaction. If the attorney was chosen based on the tenets of this book, he should be open to communication about the frustration the client is feeling and should assist the client in distinguishing between logical and emotional reactions.

Either way, the attorney and the client should be able to work it out. Clients lose credibility quickly with the Judge when they have had too many attorneys representing them on the case. Clients should always be mindful of how they are being perceived by the Judge.

7. Never mistake drama free for weakness. A common misperception is that a person who chooses a path of love and chooses to opt out of drama is weak. This mindset feeds into the oldest trick in the book for those who want to perpetuate a fight. The first thing a drama addict does, when a person is attempting to walk away, is challenge his "manhood". Call the other person a coward, call him weak, and wait for him to come back and fight to prove that you are wrong. For those addicted to drama such is a very effective tool to perpetuate chaos.

    There may be times when a countermove is necessary to get the other party's attention. When people are stuck on drama sometimes they need a wake-up call. This could be by moving out, filing a motion with the Court, etc. It is not done from a place of anger or hurt but as an act to preserve peace or sometimes to set and maintain a boundary that allows for personal growth. Sometimes a countermove is necessary to arrive at a place where conflict can truly be resolved.

    I deal with the "weakness mentality" all the time as an attorney. People assume that because you refuse to fight about senseless things that you are weak. The truth is exactly opposite. Let go of the need to constantly prove that you are strong. That need is really just a fear that you are, in fact, weak. A Divorce with Joy does not mean that you acquiesce in conflict. It doesn't mean that you lie down and let your spouse do anything or have everything she requests. It means you stand firm in a place of logic and rationality, and from a place of love, set your boundaries, stick to them resolutely but don't fight.

The most frustrating thing you can do for a person who insists on drama is disengage. I am often forced to disengage when interacting with opposing counsel. There are some attorneys who want nothing more than to argue. I cannot have an adult conversation with them. They take on their client's identity and talk to me about how worthless and evil my client is. They don't truly hear anything that is said. They play games and begin to act like a bully when they don't get their way. Does this sound familiar to you? I'll bet for many readers your spouse has behaved the same way.

Here is how I handle those attorneys. I call them on their game. When they are wasting my time, I tell them they are wasting my time. I tell them that, as long as they are wasting my time, I am no longer going to communicate with them other than by fax or email. If their emails continue the nonsense, I very politely tell them that I am not going to engage in this discussion and, no matter how many emails they send in this manner, I am not going to respond. I then sit back and watch seasoned attorneys lose their mind. I have had attorneys call my office like stalkers, three and four times a day, attempting to "talk" to me. If they wanted to truly "talk" and attempt to resolve conflict, I would absolutely talk to them. But, they don't. They want to fight. They think they can intimidate me into their client's position or they can present just the right argument to make me say, "Oh yeah, I know my 10 years of experience and knowledge of the law tells me that you are dead wrong, but I am going to go along with your point of view anyway." They are, in the truest sense of the word, control freaks.

Here is the parallel for your life. When I hit that point

with another attorney, I have made an honest, emotion-less evaluation of the case. The position that I am taking is sound, logical and well-reasoned. The Judge may ultimately determine I am wrong but I have weighed the options and know that I am making a good bet. I have checked my thought process with my trusted advisors. There is no reason to continue to fight about it. Are there issues like that in your life?

A Divorce with Joy does not mean that you and your spouse will agree on everything. It means that you are looking at the situation from this place of love, peace, understanding and reason. You make mindful decisions not motivated by fear, hate, anger or hurt. When you make that decision, it simply is. You can discuss your position without drama. You can defend it and you can certainly negotiate to a reasonable resolution. You can have an open mind to your spouse's position and determine what path forward works best for the collective whole, the family. If your spouse is not at a place where he can be rational and logical, you can wait patiently and resolutely.

You don't reward bad behavior by giving in to drama. You can allow your spouse to travel the path at his own speed. You cannot drag him along. You cannot convince him of your perspective unless he is ready to see it. You can never force someone to release drama. You simply disengage and live. You do not relent to drama, even upon temptation. When the two of you can have an adult conversation and truly problem solve, you engage. Until then you continue to take care of yourself and walk your own path. I find that, ultimately, people come around. I have even had attorneys come up to me months after we've resolved a divorce case and say something like, "I know I was being a pain on that case, my client was just driving me crazy." I appreciate the sentiment. I don't allow my clients the same power. I also don't allow other attorneys to drive me crazy. You don't have to allow your spouse to drive you crazy. A family can never be functional, married or divorced, living in drama and chaos.

When one person gets off the Drama Train, the others will eventually follow. When I disengage from an attorney who isn't behaving appropriately and just wants to fight, that is exactly what I am doing. I am exiting the Drama Train to nowhere and waiting very patiently for the attorney to come around to a rational, logical position in which we can discuss issues like adults. You can do the same with your spouse. It is not cold or uncaring. It is wise and courageous. You are, in the truest sense of the words, acting in the children's best interest.

8. Never attempt to hide assets or income. All attorneys have a duty of candor to the court. If we find out that you are hiding money and we don't bring it to the attention of the court, then we are at risk professional discipline. Attorneys on both sides, generally, have a broad authority to issue subpoenas to third parties. If opposing counsel gets an idea that you are hiding income, the attorney can begin to subpoena your friends, co-workers, boss, bank records, and so on. The attorney can really work to make your life miserable, or potentially jeopardize your employment. Also, if the Judge finds out you were dishonest, the entire case from there forward may not go well for you. You will have lost credibility with the Judge, and it will probably cost you more in the end than whatever the amount you were hiding. Family Law is a subsection in the practice of law where Judges encourage everybody, including the attorneys, to "play nice in the sandbox." Judges don't typi-cally like it when attorneys or their clients play games. No matter how much you are tempted to play dirty,

understand it is almost never worth it and it will almost always come back to haunt you. Karma is never more powerful than in a divorce.

9. Never talk to the children about the details of the divorce. This is true no matter the age of the children. There are many books and articles giving guidance on the way in which a parent can appropriately discuss the divorce with the children in general. The appropriate method varies greatly on the age of the children. But, never discuss the details of the divorce nor your emotional process through the divorce with your children. It is tempting, especially for the emotionally driven client, to want to talk about the divorce with the children. They are so angry they just ooze hatred toward the other parent. They talk to the children about the transgressions of the marriage and the positions in the divorce. They, either consciously or subconsciously, want the children to choose sides. Judges understand how very detrimental it is for the children (even teenage children) to be placed in the middle of the divorce. The children have a right to love each parent and they have no business in the issues of the divorce. Divorces are difficult for adults to process, it is impossible for children to deal with those issues. Truly, it isn't the child's problem. Those are your problems and your children are not your confidants. Process these issues through your Board of Directors. If you bring the children into the issues of the divorce, it will almost always hurt your legal case. Judges are not interested in rewarding parents who are so emotionally driven that they do harm to their children by involving them in the legal divorce.

10. Never refuse to comply with a court order. This seems obvious but people ignore court orders often. This is always

an emotional decision. The party doesn't agree with the court order (probably because the court order is based on reason and logic and the client is living in emotion and irrationality). So, the party will just refuse to comply. Sometimes the refusal isn't overt but very passive aggressive. Nevertheless, it will not end well for the client. Common examples deal with visitation and child support. The parent who disagrees with the order of visitation will refuse to take the children. Or, if the parent is being more passive aggressive, the parent will attempt to taint the children against visitation. The parent will tell the child he doesn't have to go to visitation if he doesn't want to or the parent will plan a special event during the other parent's visitation day so the child won't want to go.

With regard to support, the parent will sometimes simply refuse to pay the amount. Or, if the parent is being more passive aggressive, the parent will "lose" his job or delay bonuses or hide income so as not to have the "ability" to comply with the court order. Understand that all of these examples are emotional, irrational actions. Even if a client doesn't agree with a court order, the client is best served to follow it. The judge made the ruling for a reason, even if the client can't see it or doesn't agree with it. The client should comply unless and until the attorney can get the order changed.

At the Station

Once you have chosen an attorney appropriately and worked throughout the divorce process to separate the legal versus emotional aspects of divorce, you find that the divorce process can be drama free and relatively smooth. Know that, just because you now understand the concept, how it's implemented and how to effectively manage emotions in the divorce, it won't always be easy. You won't be perfect. I certainly wasn't. However, you will always be mindful. You are committed to curiosity about your thought process. You are committed to an evaluation of your motivations for each decision and you seek third party opinions from those who truly have your best interests at heart.

First and foremost, you are committed to being the keeper of your own happiness and personal growth. You are committed to being the best version of "you". And you work at it every day. Your life as you knew it wasn't built overnight. Your marriage didn't fall apart overnight. You are not going to be able to rebuild either overnight. It takes time and baby steps. But, with each step forward, things are a little easier. The world is a little brighter each step. Eventually, you look back and you don't recognize the person who began the process. Your children will have some pains of adjustment. But, because you are not engrossed in a fight, you can be receptive to their pains and react in a way to best help them adjust.

One day, in a future that may seem light years away but is right around the corner, you look at your children and realize they are so much better for the work you've done. You see the love and happiness in their faces and are washed with immense gratitude that you made the hard choices, that you Divorced (or not) with Joy.

BEING DIVORCED WITH JOY

MOVING FORWARD AS
A FAMILY AFTER DIVORCE

THE main tenets of this book are for those contemplating divorce. However, the tools work just as well for those who are already divorced and dealing with issues with the ex-spouse. Often I see people who are seeking to go back to court after their divorce. They have buyer's remorse and are feeling like they signed a bad deal. They may want to go back to court to modify a provision of the divorce decree or maybe they want to ask the Judge to hold the other party in contempt for not complying with one of the terms of the Final Judgment. At times, these are helpful tools and have an appropriate place in the legal system. However, they also can be invitations for unnecessary drama.

The Anatomy of the Legal Process of Modification and Contempt

There are two mechanisms, primarily, for getting into court after a divorce is final: 1) Modification or 2) Contempt. A modification is a request to change a provision of the final divorce decree. They are most often to modify timesharing, custody or support. However, courts generally have the ability to modify or enforce any term of the divorce. In most jurisdictions, the person has to prove that something major has changed since the Judge signed the divorce decree and that this change was not contemplated at the time of divorce. The closer in time you are to the divorce being final, the less likely it is that the Judge will modify the divorce decree. Contempt is the court's ability to enforce its own orders. Contempt usually requires: 1) an order from the court in the divorce that is clear; 2) that one of the parties is not following this order, and 3) that the failure to obey the order is willful.

Generally, contempt or modification is less expensive than an original divorce but not always. If a party is attempting to change custody/visitation, a modification can be just as financially and emotionally costly as an original divorce. They each begin the same way, by filing a motion. The other party is then provided a copy of the motion and the legal process has begun. Often on contempt, if the person is truly, willfully not following the court order, that person will simply come into compliance. At this point, the attorney can't really do much. If the person is in compliance by the time of hearing, the Judge may not even hear the motion.

A modification is usually a little more in depth, often requiring mediation and discovery just like an original divorce. If you are contemplating either a contempt or a modification, I encourage you to be cautious. I am an attorney and I can go to court for, basically, free. If my ex-husband is technically not following the order on several aspects, I have no intention of filing anything with the Court on these matters. Technically, I could go to court and have the Judge make him do things. But, I don't want to get on that Drama Train with him. It is just not worth it. Our children are having enough struggles adjusting to the two-household family, why in the world would I want to make it worse for them by entering another conflict in court?

The client should understand not all grievances are appropriate for Court. As a matter of fact, the vast majority are not. Even when the other parent is not following the Court's order, even when the other parent is technically "wrong", legal intervention is often not the best solution. Courts cannot mandate parenting in the way that you think it should go. You and your spouse are going to have to communicate and come up with a solution. I have seen people litigate whether a child should have surgery, whether the child should attend private school, whether the child will have her ears pierced, what the child's diet is going to entail, etc. Most often, the Courts won't provide answers to these questions.

Here is a personal example. I feel very strongly that our children should eat only the healthiest food, almost always organic. Our oldest son has some attention issues that I believe are exacerbated by processed foods, dyes, preservatives and chemicals in and on food. We choose not to medicate him, but rather, to control the symptoms with diet and other lifestyle choices. As a result, to feed the boys outside of these guidelines is, in my opinion, tantamount to abuse. It is medically irresponsible. Now, the boys' Father doesn't feel quite so strongly. Often they return from their Father's house and tell me they had "cakes" or "punch" or "insert whatever processed food that would survive a nuclear strike here". I believe this is the same as poisoning our children.

I could react to this in one of two ways. I could pick a fight with their Father. I could attempt to exert my will on him. I could refuse to allow the boys to go visit him and I could go back to court and accuse him of being a neglectful Father who refuses to act in their best interest or work to keep them healthy. (In case you can't see it, this would be the emotional reaction.) Or, I can be vigilant about their diet when they are with me. I can point out to their Father that their behavior and well-being is affected greatly when they eat those things and ask him to please be mindful of what they eat. But, I really can't do more than that. I have to accept that maybe I'm not even right. Maybe I am too vigilant and a more moderate approach is better. All I know for sure is that we have to co-parent. That means respecting his opinion. I don't like that they eat junk at his house. But, going to court to try to change it isn't the answer. I am finding, because I didn't start a war of wills with him, he is coming into my line of thinking more and more.

No matter how much you dislike your spouse or are hurt by her, you have to trust they too have the best interest of your children in mind, even when you disagree as to what exactly the best interest of your children looks like. To insist the Courts referee parenting decisions for your children is simply a ride on the Drama Train. Parents get so caught up in what they believe is "right" for their child or in a power struggle with the other party that they lose sight of what is truly best for the child. The creation of this chaos is an unrestricted ticket on the Drama Train. Even after the divorce, conflict must still be resolved with joy

New Boyfriends and Girlfriends

Even in the most amicable of divorces, it is difficult when new friends come around. Often people in divorces want to set parameters for the new friend, a checklist of sorts that the new friend has to fulfill before he can meet the children. I have found this to be a means of control and a way to maintain contact (and thereby conflict) among the parties. To illustrate the point, I give you this anecdote.

A client says to his divorce attorney, "I don't want some man that I don't know around my children. I have a right to approve of this person before he meets my children." At first, this may sound reasonable enough.

The attorney says, "Is there any reason to believe she would bring someone around who would endanger your children?

"Not really."

"Does your Wife love the children and want the best for them?"

"Yes."

"Well then maybe you should trust her to decide who she wants to date and when to introduce him to the children. I mean she chose you, right, so her judgment can't be all bad."

Silence.

Don't fault the parent who initially views the situation from this perspective. This is probably the most natural reaction of a person going through a divorce. However, it is up to the attorney to move the client in a more logical direction. Really, think about the message sent by a parent who wants to set a checklist for the other parent. The message is, "I don't trust you to act in the best interest of our children. I know what is best for them better than you do. I have better judgment." If a client believes these things, the attorney should encourage the client to evaluate his motives. Once this area is broached, it is likely to infuriate the other party. If the attorney is not challenging the client on this line of thought, the attorney may either be inexperienced or more concerned about a fight than the family. It is likely the client is simply having trouble letting go of control. Setting the client up for that kind of contact with the ex-spouse sets the pair up for future conflict.

Fast forward and imagine future conversations. "I don't want your girlfriend around the children." Why? (Hint: There is no good answer here. Short of "She is a child molester who was just released from prison," it isn't going to work.) If you have a clause dictating contact between the children and future boyfriends/girlfriends, it will apply equally to both parents. Let's be realistic, do you really want your ex-spouse telling you who you can and can't date?

Don't feel like there is no solution in Family Law. If your ex-spouse truly brings someone around who is potentially dangerous for the children, you can file a modification in almost every jurisdiction. If there is a real threat (as opposed to a parent simply having trouble letting go), the Court will intervene. Therefore, these clauses in divorces attempting to address future friends of the parents are just a bad idea. They create unnecessary drama and don't really provide any protection above and beyond that which already exists in the law because the Courts are not likely to be strong about enforcing or interpreting these clauses in an agreement.

Nonetheless, it is generally a good idea to wait one year after the divorce before introducing a new boyfriend or girlfriend to the children. When my Husband became my ex-husband, we verbally agreed that neither of us would introduce another person to the children for a year. It took him four months. In the continued spirit of being real, it sucked. For any Mother, it is difficult to see another person stepping into a motherly role for your children in any capacity. It triggers some very primal, protective feelings. That is okay; feel them and acknowledge them. Work those issues out with your Board of Directors.

So, my ex brings this woman around. He offers to allow me to meet her. I couldn't think of any scenario where that wouldn't create drama. I was curious. I wondered if she was better than me, prettier than me, skinnier than me, etc. She wondered the same about me, I am sure. She wanted to size me up. She wanted to know what kind of shoes she was trying to fill. All of that equates to drama. I resisted the urge and simply said, "I trust your judgment and trust that you would not bring anyone around the boys who wasn't good for them." Did I truly believe this? Maybe. But, my logical mind knew it is what I should believe.

As it turns out, the children love her. Here is another news-flash: That is equally difficult to swallow. One day I am hugging and loving my oldest son. He says to me, "Mommy you are just like (insert ex's girlfriend's name here)". The inside of my stomach hit my freshly polished toenails. But, I kept hugging him and smiled and said cheerfully "That is so great, Son." Oh, the things a Mother will do out of love for her children. It is tough. Often people don't know what do to with the emotions created by the introduction of a new friend and, at least subconsciously, create conflict. Especially for people who had a dysfunctional marriage, conflict is normal, natural and even comfortable. So, the client creates conflict because the client knows how to function with the ex in conflict.

An attorney with ulterior motives can take advantage of these feelings and encourage the client to flesh out these emotions in the legal system. This is especially true if there are clauses in the divorce (such as the "friend clause") that leave the parents open to future conflict. You know how drug dealers make money on the comeback? Well so do attorneys. In my opinion, attorneys who encourage these types of clauses in divorces are only setting their clients up for future conflict. Unless there is a serious safety threat to the child, Courts will not intervene to manage the new boyfriend/girlfriend situation. Clients are much better served working through these problems in therapy not the legal system.

Post Dissolution Matters – Extension of Conflict

Old habits have a powerful hold. Just because you managed a drama free divorce doesn't necessarily mean that you will not continue forward in drama. Unresolved issues will continue to rear their ugly heads until you deal with them. Often I see people who truly believe they are "over" the drama filled divorce jump back on the Drama Train.

When a client gets divorced, the client then has a document dictating his or her rights and responsibilities with regard to children, money, property and debt from that day forward. Even when attorneys do their best to draft an order or agreement to deal with every future contingency and every possible scenario, it is impossible. There will be gaps and situations where the subject matter of the final judgment is covered but following the order no longer makes sense due to the changes in circumstances of the parties. The best case scenario of the parties is that they have this order as a fall back in case they can't agree on an issue in the future, but they put it in a drawer and never look at it again because along the way they work things out. No matter how nasty the demise of the marriage, people (and parents in particular) must find a way to communicate in the future. The parties should deal with the ex-spouse unemotionally, like a business partner.

If the client finds him or herself in an attorney's office just months after a divorce to file a contempt or a modification, the client should take a serious look at his or her motivation. When people divorce, there is a void there. Often there is still love there. I find the people who fight the most during and after a divorce are the ones who have the most feelings remaining for the other party. People don't know how to process these emotions. They are angry and still in love with the other party and this comes out in a desire to fight with the other person. They extend the divorce and even rationalize ways to keep going back to court after a divorce as a means of simply continuing contact with the other party. They will often present themselves as the victim and indicate a desire to continue legal conflict because it is what is "right". There is no room for emotion or moral high ground in a divorce.

Here is an example. A couple goes through a very high-conflict divorce. It is nasty. There are allegations of abuse, stalking, hiding assets, etc. There are also young children between the parties. It becomes so nasty, in fact, that the Judge restrains the parties from talking to anybody about the divorce or the other party even after the divorce is final. This is, incidentally, extremely out of the ordinary. So several years after the divorce, the Mother comes to an attorney indicating the Father is behind on child support. The attorney immediately files a contempt motion, asking the court to compel payment, fine the Father and put him in jail. The attorney tells the client she doesn't have to put up with this, it is disrespectful, and a blatant disregard for what is right. After all, how dare he neglect the care of his children?

Thereby, the court case is reopened. The attorney gets paid what I can only imagine is a significant sum of money. And the proverbial can of worms is again opened. The attorney and the Mother assumed the worst of the Father and proceeded with a full on legal assault. The Father receives the brunt of the assault and is angry and offended that the Mother thought so poorly of him as to believe that he wouldn't properly care for his children. The Wife appears before the public and says that the amount of money paid in child support is inconsequential, less than $2,000 per month to a Mother who is a multi-millionaire. As it turns out, the Father didn't pay the child support because the parties agreed that he would have the children for the majority of the time during those months so that the Mother could complete a big project at work. The Father had the children significantly more than the final judgment mandated and he just assumed (although legally incorrectly) that since he was spending significantly more to care for the children during what would have normally been the Mother's time that he didn't have to also pay support. When he learned of his error, he immediately paid, but the Court case continued. Now, understand the attorney acted in a way that is allowable under the law. But, attorneys should be problem solvers not problem creators. This is true even when solving the problem is the less financially profitable solution for the attorney.

Here is the alternative way to handle the issue from the attorney and client's perspective. First of all, the Mother needs to realize that she is probably a drama queen, thrives on conflict and probably has unresolved feelings for her ex-husband. She is not a victim. She is perfectly capable of caring for the children herself and a Father who shares a significant portion of the load by exercising substantial timesharing is not a dead beat. This is true even though he missed a couple of payments. She should also realize that, no matter how much they give lip service to the fact that the children are shielded from the legal case and are not affected, it is simply not true. Anytime there is angst between the parents and especially when there is a fight in Court, there is fall out for the children.

Sometimes the issue about which the parents are fighting is worth the cost to the children. Sometimes it is even necessary for the children's safety or mental or emotional wellbeing. This was not. When the Mother sought the advice of an attorney on the contempt issue, the attorney should have asked questions about the circumstances of the timesharing over the months in question. The attorney should have evaluated the financial circumstances of the Mother and said, "Listen, this really is an inconsequential amount of money that we are talking about. It is really not good for the children to keep going back and forth to Court. I want to address your concerns but it makes more sense for me just to send a letter to the Father. Let's see what is going on and why he is all of a sudden not paying. It may be that with just a little communication we can solve the problem and avoid going to court."

If the attorney had followed this path, the attorney would not have been able to charge a big retainer. However, I suspect if the attorney had followed this path, the Father would've paid and the situation would've been diffused. Instead, the attorney played along with the client and inflated her desire to fight. The attorney allowed (or maybe even encouraged) her to play the victim. All the old feelings and conflict from the divorce resurfaced and, like boxers in a ring, the rounds began. It is, in my opinion, the result of a toxic attorney giving self-serving advice.

There are many other examples of when a client may just want to continue the conflict. These are situations where such continued court intervention may be legally allowable but is probably not in the best interests of the children. This is going to be an unpopular position but nevertheless, it needs to be said. The fact is, in many instances, the Father has had his head in the sand for a good portion of the marriage. He went to work, came home and checked out. Even in the progressive world in which we live, the Mother is still genetically and societally prone to do the majority of the child rearing. It is a fact that the Father, when navigating the waters of doing the kid thing alone, is not going to do it the way the Mother would. He may not even do it as well as the Mother. But, watch how this can play out in the post dissolution.

Shortly after my ex began exercising timesharing, we were discussing our youngest child's medicine regimen. As it turns out, he was giving our son anti-histamine in the morning and night. This is despite the fact that the packaging clearly outlines the dosage as once per day. I had two choices. 1) I could go back to Court, attempt to modify his visitation, because he was overmedicating the child or 2) I could have a gentle conversation with him in which I tried very hard not to be condescending but to instead help him do the right thing and, therefore, be a better Father. There are plenty of attorneys who will help a client with option 1. The attorney can pump the client up for a fight, raving about how it is a safety issue for the child, and the client would be a bad parent if he or she just let it go.

No matter how badly the other parent was as a spouse, a client should always first choose to give him the benefit of the doubt when it comes to the children. Don't let an attorney take your money because you are irrational and terrified to trust your ex to care for the child. The fact is, short of some serious neglect or intentional harm, which will almost always also have law enforcement or government agency involvement, the Court is probably not going to change the timesharing. All parents make mistakes. Sometimes they over medicate. Sometimes they give the child a food that he or she shouldn't have. Sometimes they don't watch the child and he falls in a pool, gets lost at a park, slams his hand in the door, etc. (Coincidentally, all of these have happened on either my watch or when the boys were with their Father... it is just life and it happens to all parents. I don't care what they will admit to you.) Don't use it as an opportunity to start or continue a legal fight which is probably going to be more harmful to the children than whatever the other parent is doing. I totally and completely understand that it is a terrifying realization that you will not always be there to protect, love and nurture you children. But, don't let an attorney prey on this fear.

Attempting to have the Court intervene on what is ultimately a normal mishap of parenting, even when the child is hurt or could potentially get hurt, should be reserved as the last resort. This does not mean the issue shouldn't be addressed, but there are other ways of doing it. There are parenting classes, parenting coordinators, therapists, and improving communication. When approached correctly, the other parent will often be receptive. Be careful not to insinuate that she is a bad parent or even that you can do it better.

Even if you don't believe it, fall on the sword and admit to mistakes you have made. Then open the discussion to how the two of you can collectively work better for the children and better ensure they don't get hurt. You have a common goal to ensure the child leads a more productive life. Let that goal be your focus. Here is the thing. This approach is free and much more likely to yield positive results. Believe it or not, it works. Unfortunately, people who thrive on conflict and drama will hate this solution. It actually solves the problem. If the problem is solved, what will there be to fight about? If there is no fight, what will I do with this energy? If you are stuck with this anxiety, you have more work to do. But, if you interested in drama free solutions, this is the exact approach I use when I am trying to solve a problem for a client.

When approached from a perspective without emotion or judgment, parents in general want to do what's best for the child. They just sometimes need some help figuring out what that is. Often I sit down with parents who are geared up for a fight. They assume the worst from the other parent and are locked and loaded to start pushing buttons. I approach the situation ignoring all of that. I build consensus that everybody loves the children and ask each parent to describe how he or she can make improvements. Notice you don't start with how the *other* parent can do better. This is not a blame game, no matter how much you may want to start with a pointed finger. This is how you problem solve drama free and from a place of love as divorced parents. I have seen the most emotional parents come around in the process and learn to work together. Resolving conflict from a place of reason and logic works. The Court system, on the contrary, is the least effective and most expensive method of resolving conflict after a divorce

My Happy Ever After

What does my happy ever after look like today? Well, my

parents get along. It took two decades but they can finally attend the same birthday parties for their grandchildren and do other Holidays together. They have been able to do for their grandchildren what they could never do for us. It shows me that it is possible for everyone. The way my parents once fought I could never imagine them interacting peacefully. But eventually the emotions faded. When the emotions were removed, even they could work together. This is proof that, had they productively processed their emotions when I was a child, they could have done better for us. It shows me there is hope for everyone.

I live in a home filled with love. My ex-husband and I speak five or six times a week. I call him almost every day when I pick the boys up from school and tell him how their days went. He does the same on his time. We are becoming better and better at working together. Practice makes perfect after all. We talk about the things that are going on in our personal lives with one another. We trust each other not to use each other's struggles to hurt one another or bring them up in court later. It feels like we are there for one another more today than during the marriage. I feel like we have a partnership now that is functional and productive. We do family dinners and outings. The boys see that their parents care for one another. I see a confidence and happiness in them that makes me proud.

Their father and I have disagreements all the time. Sometimes we even regress to the way we interacted early on in the separation. When that happens we go back to the tools. It seems to pass more quickly each time. It is not perfect. I don't like all of his choices. He doesn't like all of mine. Sometimes we express those feelings, sometimes we do not. Either way, we do not fight. We strive to do better for our boys each day. I have not looked at our divorce decree since it was signed. He recently asked me, "Who has Thanksgiving this year?" I said, "I don't know, but I know your only vacation is Thanksgiving Day. My office is closed Wednesday through Sunday so if you want the actual day, take it. I can do 'Thanksgiving' another day." You see, we just work it out. We try to be as flexible as possible to maximize the boys' time with each of us and help each other be the best parent we can be. That is, I think, what our children deserve.

On a personal level, I have never been happier. I have challenges and peaks and valleys but I find the same tools I used to get through the divorce work for any challenge in life. Those tools work for any period of transition. I go back to the same fundamentals anytime my life becomes unmanageable. I am a student of this life and all its beautiful lessons. "If you are to live the joyous life that you came forth to live you must allow yourself to be that which you have become." Abraham-Hicks. I have learned that I deserve a joyous life. It was always there. I was the mountain standing in my own way. The good news is that is a mountain I can move. And each day I simply try to get out of my own way. I smile often, love freely and thank God for every single experience. I am humbled to have been given the experiences I have been allowed to share in this book. This is my happy ever after.

CONCLUSION

I started writing this book towards the end of my divorce. I finished it over a year later. I struggled with how much to include. I struggled with opening up my heart and my mind for the world. At times I struggled with whether or not I should even be writing a book. After all, I've made some serious "mistakes" in my life. What do I know? I finally decided that it didn't matter what I "knew". My true education did not come from all of my degrees but from life. I decided there is power in the simple. I simply share my story, my path. I don't share with you to tell you how to live your life or what is right for you. I share with you only how I experienced my path. My intention is for this book to be equal parts practical experience and life changing ideas. Some people aren't ready to hear the life changing ideas. That is certainly okay. Maybe after reading you only take the practical application and leave the life-change. Maybe the book's only purpose for you is to begin sowing the seeds for your big life change to come in the future. Each reader will see exactly what they want to see. I can't pull you off the Drama Train if you insist on gluing yourself to the seat. All I can say is that the Drama Train didn't work for me.

Our first son was born at a time when I didn't pray very much. However, in meeting him, I felt overwhelming anxiety that I was going to mess him up. I prayed, fervently, one single prayer, "God, I will do whatever you tell me to do, but I don't want to mess him up. If I get only one thing right in life, please let it be my role as a Mother." He answered that prayer and continues to answer it every day. The ironic thing was that being a good Mother means only one singular thing, being the best, most authentic version of Me.

If I had known how hard it would be and the amount of pain I would have to feel and process along the way, I may not have been able to pray that prayer. Thank God we don't see the whole staircase in the beginning. I probably would've run the other way. I am not yet at the top of that staircase. Maybe I will never reach the top, but I continue to take steps. Some steps are forward, some are back. I am not the same person finishing this book as I was when I started. I hope that you aren't either. I've been working through a whole set of new steps on the staircase as I continue in the dating process. I suspect you'll hear all about that very soon. I have an inspiration for the next book — "Dating with Joy – Your Updated Fairytale." That experience, however, is not yet written. Until then, I wish each of you much love and healing.

With my whole heart,
Joy

Steps to Divorcing (or not) with Joy

1. Cultivate Faith – an unfailing belief, not based on proof, your family will ultimately thrive
2. Meditate and begin to develop an intimate and loving relationship with the best part of you.
3. Engage a good therapist, relationship coach, support group, pastor or psychologist — Love your children enough to fix yourself.
4. Disconnect from the fight. You cannot see clearly when all your energy is spent fighting with your spouse.
5. Stop blame and grow in a spirit of acceptance of your role in the breakdown of the marriage. You cannot change your future if you continue to be a victim of your past.
6. Let go of your quest for justice. Give grace, not because your spouse deserves it but because you and your children deserve it.
7. Clean out your mental, emotional and spiritual baggage
8. Take care of your body and your health so that you may be the most effective advocate for your children.
9. Now that you have progressed in the cleaning out process there will be a void. Fill it with good (or God if He brings you there).
10. Only after arriving at Step 10 do you decide if there is any chance your marriage can be saved. If it can, work on it feverishly. If it can't, choose an attorney to move forward

with the divorce from a place of love, rationality and understanding.

11. Be mindful of your process. Make the best choices you can each day. Give gratitude for your progress.

12. ENJOY your new life! It will get better every day. When the next problem rears its ugly head go back to step one. The destination, after all, is the journey.

The Divorce Prayer

(I encourage you to say this out loud every day.)

To My Highest Power,

I pray that you open the eyes of my heart. I pray that you help me see clearly Your path and receive Your message. I pray you soften my heart to forgiveness. I pray You guide me to change every single thing that I need to change so that my children have the best possible life. I pray you lead me to live in Your love, to reflect Your light and seek the answers only You can give. Open my heart and mind to Your Divine Will and give me Your supernatural strength to follow it. Protect all of those in my life in the process. Give me faith that my family will not just survive but thrive. With all my being, I want to see You.

In Your Holy Name,
Amen

Drama Free Pledge

I _____ on this day of _____, 20 choose to believe that there is a place for common sense and spiritual awakening in the divorce process and make the following commitments as I move through this time of transition and contemplate the future of my marriage:

- I commit to a faith, an unfailing belief, my family will come through the process happier and healthier whether, in the end, I am married or divorced.

- I commit to daily meditation.

- I commit to curiosity about myself, my thought process and my perspective. I agree to maintain an open mind about my belief system and agree to receive openly any challenge to that which I "believe."

- I agree to engage the services of a therapist and timely complete all tasks the therapist requests, no matter how uncomfortable.

- I agree to stop pointing the finger, or placing blame, on my spouse, on the legal system or any other person in my life. I agree to engage in an accounting of my own role in arriving at this point and take responsibility for my own actions.

- I agree to systematically engage in a breakdown. I agree to break down each aspect of my personality, character, world view, and behavior and rebuild it in a way that is happier and healthier in which my children can live in love.

- I agree to refrain from fighting with my spouse, no matter how tempting or how much anger and hostility I feel. If need be, I agree only to communicate with my spouse through email or text and I agree to keep the communication business-like and mature.

- If I choose to move forward with divorce, I agree to choose an attorney out of love. I agree to thoroughly research my attorney and be mindful I am not making any choices from a place of anger or desperation. I agree to allow my attorney to challenge me on the emotional versus legal aspects of a divorce. I agree to address emotional issues only in a therapeutic process and legal issues only in the legal process.

- I agree to always act in my children's best interest and place their needs above any negative feeling I may have through the process.

- Lastly, I commit to being a good steward of my happiness.

To these things I commit with my whole heart, mind and spirit,

_____

Made in the USA
Las Vegas, NV
24 May 2021

23566018R00098